Achiev

Learning and Teaching in Secondary Schools

Second edition

edited by Viv Ellis

Learning Matters

For Angela's 22-year commitment to Woodway

First published in 2002 by Learning Matters Ltd.
Reprinted in 2002.
Reprinted in 2003 (twice).
Second edition published in 2004.
Reprinted in 2004, 2005 (twice) and 2006.

British Library Cataloguing in Publication Data
A CIP record for this book is available from the British Library.

ISBN-13: 978 1 844450 04 6
ISBN-10: 1 844450 04 X

The right of Rob Batho, Jane Briggs, Sue Brindley, Alan J. Child, John Clay, Viv Ellis, Patrick Fullick, Rosalyn George, Gary D. Kinchin, Kate Mackrell, Chris Matcham, Geraldine A. Price and Cathy Wickens to be identified as an author of this work has been asserted by them in accordance with the Copyright, Designs and Patents Act 1988.

Cover design by Topics – The Creative Partnership
Project management by Deer Park Productions
Typeset by PDQ Typesetting, Newcastle under Lyme
Printed and bound by Bell & Bain Ltd, Glasgow

Learning Matters Ltd
33 Southernhay East
Exeter EX1 1NX
Tel: 01392 215560
Email: info@learningmatters.co.uk
www.learningmatters.co.uk

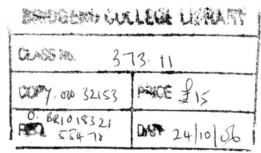

Achieving QTS
Learning and Teaching in Secondary Schools

CONTENTS

There is website support for the second edition at:
www.learningmatters.co.uk/education/learnteach.html

Rob Batho, Key Stage 3 National Strategy ITT Senior Regional Director.

Jane Briggs (formerly Treacher), Senior Lecturer in Education, University of Brighton.

Sue Brindley, Lecturer in Education, University of Cambridge.

Alan J. Child, Key Stage 3 National Strategy Regional Director (Behaviour and Attendance).

John Clay, Senior Inspector for Ethnic Minority Achievement, London Borough of Greenwich.

Viv Ellis, University Lecturer in Educational Studies, University of Oxford.

Patrick Fullick, Lecturer in Education, University of Southampton.

Rosalyn George, Senior Lecturer in Education, Goldsmiths College, University of London.

Gary D. Kinchin, Senior Lecturer in Physical Education and Secondary PGCE Director, University of Southampton.

Kate Mackrell, formerly Senior Lecturer and Visiting Lecturer in Education at the Universities of Brighton and East London.

Chris Matcham, Assistant Headteacher, Woodway Park School and Community College, Coventry.

Geraldine A. Price, Lecturer in Specific Learning Difficulties, University of Southampton.

Cathy Wickens, Senior Lecturer in ICT Education, University of Brighton.

Acknowledgements

The editor and contributors would like to thank the following people for their support and assistance in the development of this book:

Ruth Butler and Dave Simpson for their contributions to Chapter 3; David Minford; Keith Jones; the PGCE secondary English group at the University of Brighton (2000 – 2001); Ed Podesta; Maggie Miller; Deb Davies; Nathalie Manners; Rachel Norridge; staff and students at Woodway Park School and Community College; the anonymous reviewers who contributed to the development of this second edition.

This book was written for anyone undertaking a course of training leading to Qualified Teacher Status (QTS) for the secondary (11–18) phase. If this applies to you, then you may be registered at a university or college on an undergraduate degree programme with QTS, you may be taking a Post Graduate Certificate of Education (PGCE) course, or you may be following one of the employment-based routes to QTS such as the Graduate Teacher or Overseas Trained Teacher programmes. Whatever the particular route, you will be based in schools for most of your time and working with tutors and mentors towards the same goal: becoming an effective new teacher and achieving the Professional Standards for the Award of QTS. This book offers you useful guidance and support during the process of becoming a secondary teacher and shows how the information and guidance it provides relates to the QTS Standards.

The title of this book is *Learning and Teaching in Secondary Schools*. Our intention here is to emphasise the *learning* for two reasons: first, to acknowledge that this is what you – the trainee teacher – will be engaged in for a significant period and with some intensity. For this reason, the book addresses you directly, provides some classroom-based illustrations, and offers practical tasks and further reading to consolidate your understanding. The second reason is that fostering, developing, assessing, planning for and managing student learning is what your primary role is as a teacher. This may sound obvious but very often trainee teachers will initially focus on the performance aspects of teaching – how teachers look, behave and sound – rather than how and what their students are learning. We hope you will find it reassuring when we say that very good teachers do not need to be extrovert or overtly 'charismatic' performers; very good teachers listen to students carefully, think about what they see, hear and read analytically and treat students and colleagues with sensitivity. You don't need to be a Mr Keating (from the film *Dead Poets' Society*) – with a flamboyant, physical style or an understated taste in tweed – or any of the other examples from film and television to be a highly successful classroom teacher.

Learning to teach

Becoming a teacher is a rewarding, stimulating and challenging process. Do not underestimate the changes in your life and circumstances that may occur during this process! This is not to say that undertaking a course leading to QTS will inevitably lead to divorce, stress-related illness or the decision to keep a small-holding on Skye. It is fair to say, however, that the process of becoming a teacher involves personal, intellectual and professional transformation and that, for many trainees, it requires them to consider what is important and meaningful to them for the first time. As a consequence, most trainees feel that – at the end of their initial training – not only have they learned a lot about teaching and learning but they have also learned a lot about themselves. For most, this acts as confirmation of their initial desire to teach and confirms that they have entered a profession that they will find rewarding. For some, however, whether early on or at the end of the course, it will confirm that teaching is not for them. This is an important decision that carries with it no sense of failure.

One of the best writers about the process of becoming a teacher is the American psychologist Seymour Sarason and his book *You Are Thinking of Teaching?* is recommended as further reading at the end of this introduction. Sarason's point is that any decision to enter the teaching profession must be an informed one: you must understand why you want to become a teacher *and* what it means to be a teacher (the responsibilities and the constraints):

> If you conclude that teaching is for you, it should be on the basis that you know who and what you are, the ways in which you will be challenged, and that you are prepared to be other than a silent, passive participant in the socially fateful and crucial effort to improve our schools; that is, the particular school or schools in which you work.
>
> (Sarason 1993, p. 4)

In addition to knowing why you want to become a teacher and that you understand its active and socially important role, Sarason also draws attention to the 'political' dimension of teaching, a dimension with which you might feel uncomfortable. Couched in the following terms, however, it is difficult to disagree with the view that teachers effect this kind of change:

> It is unfair and unrealistic to expect teachers to change the society. It is not unfair or unrealistic to expect teachers to change, in part if not wholly, the conditions in which they and their students experience personal and intellectual growth.
>
> (*ibid.*, p. 5)

The new Professional Standards for the Award of QTS, by placing Professional Values and Practice before anything else, recognise that this kind of change is at the heart of the teacher's role.

The current context for teacher education and training

All aspects of the education system in the UK have been subject to rapid and substantial change for at least 15 years. The pace of change can be bewildering and can leave some teachers feeling disoriented. As a new trainee, you will also be faced with new initiatives and further change but it is perhaps fair to say that many significant changes will have started to 'bed down' by the time you become a newly-qualified teacher. Teachers and teacher trainers have already struggled with the demands of Curriculum 2000, Standards-based teacher training and much of the Key Stage 3 National Strategy. Of the new developments, you are most likely to experience significant change in two: some aspects of the Key Stage 3 National Strategy and the 14–19 curriculum.

Key Stage 3 National Strategy

There are six strands in the Strategy. These are:

1. English (including Literacy across the curriculum);
2. Mathematics (including Numeracy across the curriculum);
3. Science;
4. ICT (Information and Communications Technology);
5. Foundation subjects;
6. Behaviour and attendance.

The English and Mathematics strands of the Key Stage 3 National Strategy were introduced to all schools in England in 2001 with science, foundation subjects and ICT following in 2002 and behaviour and attendance in 2003. The aim of the Strategy is to raise standards by strengthening teaching and learning across the curriculum for all pupils aged 11 to 14. Literacy is one of the cross-curricular elements of the Strategy.

All secondary trainees will need to be familiar with the cross-curricular elements of the Strategy as well as any strand that applies to their specialist subject. During your time in schools, you will undoubtedly be part of training that is related to the Strategy. Its main principles are concerned with improving learning and teaching in the classroom and can be summarised as follows.

SET HIGH EXPECTATIONS AND GIVE EVERY LEARNER CONFIDENCE THEY CAN SUCCEED
- Demonstrate a commitment to every learner's success, making them feel included, valued and secure.
- Raise learners' aspirations and the effort they put into learning and engage, where appropriate, the active support of parents or carers.

ESTABLISH WHAT LEARNERS ALREADY KNOW AND BUILD ON IT
- Set clear and appropriate learning goals, explain them, and make every learning experience count.
- Create secure foundations for subsequent learning.

STRUCTURE AND PACE THE LEARNING EXPERIENCE TO MAKE IT CHALLENGING AND ENJOYABLE
- Use teaching methods that reflect the material to be learned, match the maturity of the learners and their learning preferences, and involve high levels of time on task.
- Make creative use of the range of learning opportunities available, within and beyond the classroom, including e-learning.

INSPIRE LEARNING THROUGH PASSION FOR THE SUBJECT
- Bring the subject alive.
- Make it relevant to learners' wider goals and concerns.

MAKE INDIVIDUALS ACTIVE PARTNERS IN THEIR LEARNING
- Build respectful teacher/learner relationships that take learners' views and experience fully into account as well as data on their performance.
- Use assessment for learning to help learners assess their work, reflect on how they learn, and inform subsequent planning and practice.

DEVELOP LEARNING SKILLS AND PERSONAL QUALITIES
- Develop the ability of learners to think systematically, manage information, learn from others and help others learn.
- Promote learners' confidence, self-discipline and an understanding of the learning process.

To be successful, the strategy depends upon teachers – and trainee teachers like yourself – using and interpreting its principles, guidance and materials in ways that are focused on improving learning and teaching in the classroom. In order to be able to do this, the core of your initial teacher training will focus upon the fundamental principles underlying learning and teaching in your specialist subject. For up-to-date information on the Strategy, go to the Department for Education and Skills Standards website at **www.standards.dfes.gov.uk/keystage3/** In addition, Chapters 6, 7 and 8 of this book address three key cross-curricular strands of the Key Stage 3 Strategy.

The 14–19 curriculum

At the time of preparing the second edition of this book, proposals were made to restructure the 14–19 curriculum in the light of the Key Stage 3 National Strategy, changes to the post-16 curriculum and the desire to increase choice and flexibility in what is currently GCSE provision and beyond. There is potential here for radical change that may have a profound impact upon the way we organise our schools and colleges. This is dealt with in more detail in Chapter 9 of this book, but for up-to-date information, go to the Qualifications and Curriculum Authority (QCA) website at **www.qca.org.uk/ca/14-19/** and the website for the Tomlinson working group at **www.14-19reform. gov.uk**

How to use this book

The chapters in this book are presented in what we hope is a logical and progressive sequence. The problem, of course, is that none of you and none of your courses will necessarily progress through the same sequence. All we can say, then, is that by starting with a chapter on professional values and ending with a chapter that looks at research, we are not implying that you will never consider professional values again after the first few weeks nor that you must postpone any understanding of the importance of research until the end of the course. Far from it; all aspects of becoming a teacher – indeed, all sections of the Standards – are interrelated.

Each chapter is prefaced by a short statement that references the content of the chapter to the Professional Standards for the Award of QTS. You will notice that the Standards are divided into three sections:

1. Professional Values and Practice;
2. Knowledge and Understanding;
3. Teaching.

Of the three sections, this book focuses on the first, Professional Values and Practice, and the third, Teaching Standards. Some chapters – particularly those addressing the cross-curricular elements of the Key Stage 3 Strategy and special educational needs – do refer to the Knowledge and Understanding section but the main focus in these Standards is on your specialist subject, how children make progress in this subject and your understanding of your subject's development in the primary phase. This subject-specific understanding is outside the remit of this book.

Additionally, the Teaching Standards are divided into three sub-sections:

3.1 Planning, expectations and targets;
3.2 Monitoring and assessment;
3.3 Teaching and class management.

You will notice that a chapter may reference across all three Standards areas and that some Standards are referenced more than once. This is the nature of teaching and of learning to teach: they are not activities that can be atomised or isolated within the whole of what teachers really do in classrooms.

How to trace important issues through the book

You will notice that the book uses the graphical device (c/r) to indicate a cross-reference to another chapter of the book. Again, this is due to the interrelationship of each aspect of learning to teach and teachers' work in classrooms. So, for example, you will see that issues of differentiation (how teachers meet individual students' needs by varying the task, the way of teaching, the use of additional support, etc) will appear in a number of chapters, including those that look at planning and inclusion. You can use the cross-reference device to trace an issue through the book when consolidating your understanding of certain key issues.

Classroom stories

Some chapters also contain 'classroom stories' that illustrate aspects of the content of the chapter in a classroom context. In Chapter 4, for example, some of the principles of formative assessment are illustrated in a dialogue between teacher and student. The 'classroom stories' are not meant to be exemplary templates or models to be imitated, however. They are examples of individual cases and fully enmeshed in a particular context. You will find them useful as cases when formulating your own ways into teaching.

Practical tasks

Each chapter includes a number of practical tasks. You can use these tasks in a number of ways.

- **To explore the relationship between the general principles outlined in the chapter and the policy of the schools in which you are training.**
- **To develop and consolidate your understanding of important skills or issues.**
- **To connect the principles informing your initial training and the practice of particular schools.**

You may find that the tasks would be a useful focus for some of the on-going work with your mentor.

There is a supplementary website to support this second edition. The website contains case studies written by trainees, files to download, links and further guidance.

The structure and content of the book

This book arises out of the contributors' work in teacher education over many years and in many different contexts. Throughout, it is informed by recent and relevant research and scholarship, including evidence from inspections and surveys by the Office for Standards in Education (Ofsted). The principles discussed in each chapter have not emerged from the ether; they have grown out of a body of evidence built by teachers and researchers over many years. In learning to be a teacher, you should not see any division between theory and practice. This is a fallacy. Even the most apparently common sense approaches to teaching are informed by a view of learning and teaching that is a theory. Effective teachers do not perform random acts; effective teachers do not simply apply the same 'solution' to every 'problem'. Underlying what effective teachers do are a set of principles that allow them to deal with very different learners in very different contexts. The development of such a set of principles in each trainee will be the aim of any course of initial training. This is part of becoming a professional.

Most of the 12 chapters in this book have been arranged into broad sections. The exceptions are Chapters 1 and 12. In Chapter 1, Fullick outlines a view of a profession and professional values and practice that refers to the standards of other professions. Much of what Fullick has to say is echoed in the chapters that follow and, indeed, the book is founded upon the assumption of the teacher as 'professional', something which is explained in this chapter. In Chapter 12, Brindley gives an overview of debates about educational research and the vital connections between how we learn, what teachers do, how teachers develop and how research informs policy and practice. As with Chapter 1, the themes of this chapter – especially the view that all teachers are engaged in intellectual inquiry – are reflected throughout the book.

Chapters 2 to 5 are concerned primarily with learning and how you as a trainee will learn to take account of individual students' needs, to plan for and assess learning, and to manage all this within the classroom setting. The contributions by Kinchin, Ellis, Briggs and Child should be seen as an inter-related suite of chapters.

Chapters 6 to 9 cover important issues of curriculum and teaching. Chapters 6 to 8 (Batho, Mackrell and Wickens) address three important (cross-curricular) strands of the Key Stage 3 National Strategy. These chapters contain proportionately more practical tasks than the others and sometimes refer to the Strategy training materials that will be available in your schools. They also cover key teaching strategies that will be useful to trainees of all subjects. Chapter 9 (Matcham) discusses the proposals to change the curriculum for 14- to 19-year-olds and some of the cross-curricular issues post-14. Again, there are practical tasks to allow you to develop your understanding of this area in relation to your own subject.

Chapters 10 (Price) and 11 (Clay and George) cover the core issue of inclusion. The principles of inclusion are at the heart of the National Curriculum and other legislation that applies to schools and to teachers. Price offers a coherent overview of the special educational needs area, including specific learning difficulties and working with other adults to support learning. Clay and George discuss the broader inclusive issues of gender, 'race' and social class and how these impact on the work of teachers. Both chapters return to the themes of Chapters 1 and 12 and support the view that inclusion is a core professional value for all teachers.

Reading this book and engaging with the practical tasks alone will not enable you to become an effective teacher and to demonstrate achievement against the QTS Standards. This book can only support the intensive and interactive training you undertake as part of your course in schools and in higher education. The Professional Standards for the Award of QTS offer training providers – universities, colleges, local authorities and schools – the opportunity to design courses that regard teacher development holistically rather than as the 'ticking off' of separate competences that need to be 'evidenced' in wheel-barrows full of paper. Such courses acknowledge that values and dispositions (towards young people, to learning, to society, to teaching as a profession, etc) accompanied by an understanding of how we learn and how we promote and assess learning, together with delight in a particular subject or subjects, and combined with skills of planning, organisation and communication are what effective teaching is all about. The contributors offer this book in support of such training programmes.

Further reading

Sarason, S.B. (1993) *You Are Thinking of Teaching? Opportunities, Problems, Realities*. San Francisco. Jossey-Bass. This is one of the best books available on the reasons why (or why not) to become a teacher. Sarason discusses the challenges that new teachers face in many aspects of their lives. He also explores issues of change in the lives of more experienced teachers. Although difficult to find in some libraries, this book is worth locating.

Smith, J. (2002) *The Learning Game: A Teacher's Inspirational Story*. London. Abacus. Jonathan Smith has taught for many years at an independent school in Kent. This book is part memoir, part guide to becoming a teacher and keeping a sense of balance in your life. Although you are likely to be learning to teach in a very different context, this is an enjoyable and thought-provoking book.

1 PROFESSIONAL VALUES AND THE TEACHER

PATRICK FULLICK

Professional Standards for QTS

 1.1–1.8

To be awarded QTS you must have high expectations of all your students, respect their social, cultural, linguistic, religious and ethnic backgrounds, and be committed to raising their educational achievement. You should be able to demonstrate that you treat students respectfully and consistently and are concerned for their development as learners. You should promote the positive behaviour and attitudes that you expect from your students.

You must be able to communicate with parents and carers clearly and sensitively, recognising their roles in students' learning, and their rights, responsibilities and interests in this. You should be committed to sharing and participating in the corporate life of your school.

You should show an understanding of the contribution of support staff and other professionals to teaching and learning, as well as being able to improve your own teaching, by evaluating it, learning from the effective practice of others and from evidence. You should take increasing responsibility for your own professional development.

You should be familiar with the statutory frameworks relating to teachers' responsibilities.

You may find it helpful to read through the appropriate section of the handbook that accompanies the Standards for the Award of QTS for clarification and support.

Introduction

What do people think about teachers?

So you've decided that you want to teach … the contributors to this book are very pleased to hear it. But why teaching? It may seem rather strange to suggest to student teachers that they should begin their course by asking themselves this question, but as I hope you'll soon see, there are some very good reasons for doing so. Before we begin the process of reflecting on reasons for wanting to teach, let's look at what some people have said about teachers and teaching.

- A man who knows a subject thoroughly, a man so soaked in it that he eats it, sleeps it, dreams it, this man can always teach it with success, no matter how little he knows of technical pedagogy. (H. L. Mencken)
- For every person wishing to teach, there are 30 not wishing to be taught. (W. C. Sellar)

- He who can, does. He who cannot, teaches. (George Bernard Shaw)
- It was God who made me beautiful. If I weren't, then I'd be a teacher. (Linda Evangelista)
- He was my favourite teacher in the school. If he hadn't been at the school, I don't think I would have been that clever. He's told me everything that I really want to know. (Teacher Training Agency publicity)

Practical task

Think about each of the statements above. You may be able to add others about teaching that you have come across. Each statement carries a message about teachers and teaching.

- *Write down two or three sentences setting out what you think lies behind each statement.*
- *Now write two or three sentences setting out what these statements say to you about your choice of teaching as a career. A possible starting point for this is to think about what kind of reasoned response you would make to someone who made one of these statements to you.*

If you have the opportunity, discuss your reactions to these statements with other beginning teachers, and with experienced teachers too. To what extent do you think stereotypical views of teachers are inevitable? Are such stereotypes necessarily a bad thing?

Of course, I have been highly selective in the quotations I have chosen to use – whenever we teach we use quotations and examples that will support the ideas we are trying to convey! But these quotations illustrate a number of things that have been said to me, or to my colleagues and my students, in my years as a teacher educator. The overall gist of these is:

- to be a successful teacher, you've got to know your subject well;
- which will make teaching it pretty easy;
- although you'll still have to deal with a lot of kids who just don't want to know;
- so maybe teaching is something that you do if you haven't got anything better to do;
- although if you're successful, it can be quite a fulfilling job.

If you find these messages about teachers and teaching a bit confusing, then you find yourself in the same position as most seasoned teachers and educators. In my experience, it does not get less confusing when we look outside my (selective) quotations at the messages coming to us from the media, from friends and colleagues – most of these sources provide a great mixture of ideas about what teachers and teaching are all about. Just why this is the case could form the basis of a whole book in its own right. But for the moment I want to encourage you to think about the following points.

- **Although adults are often unclear about what they expect of teachers, students are much less so.**

- Teachers need to be clear about the expectations that other people have of them in order to behave appropriately.
- Teachers also need to be clear about the expectations they have of themselves as part of the process of deciding how to behave.
- Codes of behaviour and professional standards set out by government and by professional bodies are necessary starting points for deciding on one's own personal, professional standards of behaviour – but they are insufficient on their own.

In thinking about these points, you will not necessarily come to any quick and simple answers, but you will have begun an important process, involving a journey towards a set of personal professional values that are rooted in your own beliefs and values, as well as in what other people require of you.

Expectations – adults vs children

At first sight it seems surprising that there should be so much confusion about people's expectations of teachers. After all, teachers are a set of people of whom we all have experience at some point in our lives, and most people probably feel that they are pretty clear about just what it is that teachers do and how they should behave – their *professional ethics*. In a review article, Haydon (1996:301) points out that the term *professional ethics* is 'more likely to bring to mind issues about the practice and attitudes of lawyers or doctors than of teachers in schools', noting that there is 'a lack of certainty or clarity about the status of teaching as a profession'. In a lengthy discussion following these points, Haydon compares the activities of teachers with those of other professionals such as doctors and lawyers. What seems to give rise to the confusion about teaching is that, while most people can reasonably readily agree about the 'good ends' that professionals like doctors and lawyers pursue (in the case of doctors, health, and in the case of lawyers, justice), people are generally much less clear about the 'good end' pursued by teachers – education – even though it can be argued that health and justice are not, in themselves, necessarily straightforward concepts.

Whatever the source of the confusion, at this point in deciding on your own professional values there is little that you can do other than to acknowledge it, and then move on. But while adults as a whole may be unclear about the kind of values they expect teachers to have, there is evidence to suggest that among students there is a fair degree of agreement about the values that teachers should have. In addition, teachers themselves are also in general agreement about these values, while the same evidence also provides some support for the idea that teachers and their students agree quite closely about values; and not only those values that should apply to teachers, but those that should apply to students too.

Research in the area of teachers' values is rather thin on the ground. In those empirical studies that do exist, one interesting strategy employed both with children and with student teachers, is the use of drawing. Coming from the field of cultural studies, research methods involving drawing are based on the idea that 'writing paints pictures with words, while drawings speak with lines and colours' (Weber and Mitchell

1996:304). Such methods have been widely used by researchers exploring such diverse things as children's images of scientists (Tuckey 1992) and what it means to be healthy (Wetton and McWhirter 1998).

Practical task

Before reading on, take time to think about how you see yourself as a teacher. Now draw a picture to answer the questions 'How do you see yourself as a teacher?' (Don't worry about how good your drawing is technically – the ideas it's conveying are the important thing!) If possible, carry out this task among a group of student teachers who are at the same stage of their professional development as you. Share your drawing with each other and discuss what they convey. What similar ideas do you have? What ideas are different?

How do your drawings compare to those in Figures 1 and 2?

Weber and Mitchell's research was carried out with student teachers on courses in the USA, producing a diversity of images with strong themes of 'nurturing' and 'controlling' running throughout. (See Figures 1 and 2.) As well as a research tool, Weber and Mitchell see drawing as a means of helping student teachers reflect on and explore their conceptualisation of their developing ideas about how they see themselves as a teacher during their course.

Figure 1: A traditional portrayal of a teacher (from Weber and Mitchell 1996:306).

Figure 2: A non-traditional portrayal of a teacher (from Weber and Mitchell 1996:306).

Children's drawings of teachers like these share a number of common features (see Figures 3 and 4), most notably their bright (smart?) clothing and a big smile. For Wetton and McWhirter, the presence of a smile in an image of a person drawn in response to the instruction 'Draw a healthy person' indicates the need for mental health as part of overall healthiness. However, researchers exploring images of teachers are less certain about the meaning of a smile in a drawing of a teachers' face:

Figure 3: Mrs Richards by Sophie D, 4R
(from Porth Junior School, 2000).

Figure 4: Mr Morris by Carys B, 4R
(from Porth Junior School, 2000).

What does a smile signify? Surely the female teachers' smiles are intended to indicate good will, a lack of threatening intent. But a smile, as it is often unconsciously practiced [sic] by females, also signifies a lack of threat that may be interpreted as a submissive attitude, a desire to please. Why do the male teachers not need to smile so continuously? Does this reflect male and female socialization, and if so, what does it mean for the role of female teachers both in the classroom and in the larger contexts of school and society?

(Trousdale 1994 quoted in Weber and Mitchell 1996, p.311)

While draw-a-teacher research provides some insight into teachers' values, text-based research provides insights into the extent to which students and teachers share ideals. Researchers in Finland (Verkasalo *et al* 1996) administered a questionnaire to 428 15-year-old students and 134 of their teachers. Analysis of the responses showed that both teachers and pupils were in close agreement as to the values that an ideal teacher should display – especially highly rated were:

- **benevolence (incorporating such ideals as loyalty, honesty, helpfulness, responsibility and forgiveness);**
- **and universalism (broad-mindedness, social justice, equality, world at peace, unity with nature).**

There was less agreement about the values held by students. Students were asked to rate the values that they regarded as most important for *themselves* and for *an ideal student*. Answers to these questions showed that students felt that values which they regarded as the most important for themselves (true friendship, freedom, meaning in life and sense of belonging) were not the same as the most important values that an ideal student should hold. However, teachers also saw the students' personal values as very important in an ideal student. This means that we have the interesting situation that, while teachers and students are broadly in agreement about the values held by ideal teachers, students do not see their own values as being those of an ideal student, although teachers do ascribe these values to ideal students!

Although this research has not been replicated in the UK, another study with teachers only (Walker and Newman 1995) shows that teachers hold a large number of values in common when asked to rate agreement or disagreement with statements about teaching.

Expectations – what are yours?

We began thinking about developing a set of values to guide you through the early part of your teaching career by posing the question 'What do people think about teachers?'. Having given this some thought, and looked at the kinds of expectations placed on teachers by others (adults and children) and by themselves, as part of the process of clarifying your own values I should now like to invite you to consider your reasons for wanting to teach.

'Why teach?'

Whatever your answer to this question, I suggest that it is possible to classify it into one of six different 'teacher portraits', as follows (I am grateful to my colleague Mike Smith for these portraits, and for their descriptions):

- **'it pays the rent/mortgage';**
- **the missionary;**
- **the imitator;**
- **the child;**
- **the bully;**
- **the radical.**

Let's look at each of these in turn.

'IT PAYS THE RENT'

While no-one denies a teacher's right to be fairly remunerated, the idea that the job of a teacher can be viewed purely as an economic transaction (labour in exchange for money) is one that is difficult to sustain. Being a professional carries responsibilities, and the role of a teacher is not one that is susceptible to the simple equation x hours of labour = y amount of money. A professional approach to the job is therefore some-thing that must be at the heart of every teacher's set of values.

THE MISSIONARY

At an early stage in their career, many teachers want to act as a shining example to others, both as a person and as a professional. Yet in the messy world of schools and teaching many compromises are necessary, which can lead to disillusionment. While initial missionary zeal may not necessarily turn to cynicism in every case, every teacher needs to be able to temper their ideals in the short term in order to achieve what they set out to do in the longer term.

THE IMITATOR

As we set out to become teachers nearly all of us will have someone in mind who inspired us in the past. It is all too easy to remember that great teacher who taught us as students and to seek to become 'just like them' – the problem is, you're not them. For one thing, you are working at a different time to them, and almost certainly in a different setting. You have a different set of skills and characteristics to them (no matter how much training you do), and you have a completely different set of experiences.

THE CHILD

If we're lucky we have many happy memories of our own childhoods. In order to work with young people effectively we need to move on from childhood and leave childish things behind. The teacher who seeks to relate to children as a friend is on dangerous ground – in more ways than one. Leaving the legal aspects of teacher-student relationships aside, students need a teacher who is able to guide, to offer explanations and to encourage. To do this teachers need to develop a professional relationship with students that is based on respect, but which is not simply a meeting of equals. Never confuse being friendly (good) with being a friend (bad).

THE BULLY

While it is not appropriate here to explore what makes someone a bully, there is a fine line between being assertive and being a bully. There will be many occasions when you will need all your powers of persuasion to convince a class that what you are asking them to do is reasonable – be it to discuss a Shakespearean sonnet on a wet Friday afternoon, or to solve a maths problem for homework. While we may feel that we need to 'bully' children into doing things, we should never do this on the basis of abusing the power that we have as teachers, either as an authority figure or as a person who is older and/or bigger than our students. Any coercion has to be based on our own enthusiasm, to persuade students that they can and should achieve something, and that to do so is both good and desirable, even if it does not seem to be so in the short term.

THE RADICAL

While many of us may come into teaching wishing to change the world, there is a world of difference between encouraging discussion and debate among our pupils and fomenting revolution. While all teachers should feel that they have the duty (and not just the right) to encourage debate of controversial issues in their classrooms, to lead that debate by encouraging students to formulate a particular view is something that lies outside the remit of the teacher. Learn to make it clear to students when you are expressing a personal view about something – and to make it clear to them that other people may hold different views. Better still, ensure that they are able to hear more than one side of any argument that may excite particularly strong feelings.

Your reasons for teaching

As you think about these portraits, many of you may find yourselves thinking 'but my reasons for teaching are like that ...' or something similar. I certainly do not want to argue here that none of these reasons for wanting to teach is valid, or that any of them alone accurately represents a viewpoint that aspiring teachers necessarily hold. However, I do believe that any of these portraits, taken on its own, represents a seriously deficient model for a teacher to have, and encourage you to think more widely. In particular, you should be very clear about your motivation for teaching, whether you see it rooted within your subject, or within a desire to work with young people. Hopefully by this point you are beginning to think in terms of visualising the teacher as someone whose desire to teach comes from both of these sources – you will certainly need a good understanding of your subject to teach it at secondary level, and it will be a difficult job to do if you don't like your students.

Practical task

Take time to think about your reasons for wanting to teach. No doubt you wrote about this on the form when you applied for your course, and it was certainly explored at interview with your tutors. At some point in your career someone is bound to ask 'what do you teach?' when they find out that you are a secondary teacher. If you reply 'maths' (or whatever your subject is) they might say 'but what about children – don't you care about them?'. On the other hand, if you say 'children' they might say 'but what about your subject – isn't that important to you?'. What will you say?

Professional frameworks

For anyone seeking to be awarded the status of a qualified teacher in England, it is necessary to be able to demonstrate the ability to meet the requirements of the government document Qualifying to Teach (DfES 2002) – and in this chapter we are concerned with the statements relating to Professional Values and Practice in the document. As I hope you will already have gathered, my point to you as beginning teachers is that you should see the values contained in these standards as a statement of what you have to do in order to achieve QTS rather than a set of values *in their own right*. I have tried to set out the reason for this in what has gone before in this chapter – that every teacher needs to understand the basis of their own professional values and those of their colleagues, and to have some idea about from where they are derived. This is not to question the values in the Standards document – but we do need to be clear about these values in order to make them our own. It is also important that we do this to ensure that we abide with values in the Standards not just in the detail of what they say but also in the spirit of their meaning.

Other professions have had codes of behaviour for a very long time – most people will be familiar with the Hippocratic Oath of the medical profession, for example. Derived from this oath, the General Medical Council has produced a document called 'The Duties of a Doctor', which is reproduced below. Effectively this is the equivalent of the values in 'Qualifying to Teach'.

The duties of a doctor registered with the General Medical Council

Patients must be able to trust doctors with their lives and well-being. To justify that trust, we as a profession have a duty to maintain a good standard of practice and care and to show respect for human life. In particular as a doctor you must:

- **make the care of your patient your first concern;**
- **treat every patient politely and considerately;**
- **respect patients' dignity and privacy;**
- **listen to patients and respect their views;**
- **give patients information in a way they can understand;**
- **respect the rights of patients to be fully involved in decisions about their care;**
- **keep your professional knowledge and skills up to date;**
- **recognise the limits of your professional competence;**
- **be honest and trustworthy;**
- **respect and protect confidential information;**
- **make sure that your personal beliefs do not prejudice your patients' care;**
- **act quickly to protect patients from risk if you have good reason to believe that you or a colleague may not be fit to practise;**
- **avoid abusing your position as a doctor;**
- **work with colleagues in the ways that best serve patients' interests.**

In all these matters you must never discriminate unfairly against your patients or colleagues. And you must always be prepared to justify your actions to them. (Available at **www.gmc-uk.org/standards/standards.frameset.htm**)

Practical task

Compare the values in 'Qualifying to Teach' with those in 'The Duties of a Doctor'.

1. *Doctors' 'clients' are their patients – who is the 'client' in the case of teachers?*

2. *Doctors have to respect patients' confidential information – what duties do teachers have in the case of information about students?*

3. *Patients have rights to be involved in decisions about their care – what rights attach to decisions about students?*

4. *What other values are present in 'Qualifying to teach', and what are their equivalents for doctors?*

While the professional standards for teachers are demanding, I have every confidence that hard work and diligence during your course will mean that you will have no problems in meeting the standards, and in setting a fine example, both professionally and personally. As you reflect on and evaluate your practice during the course, return to the Standards and to the ideas about your own values that you have thought about as you have read this chapter. Ask yourself 'Is this how I would wish others (students, parents, colleagues) to see me, and to think of me?' If the answer is 'yes' – well done! If not – why not?

Professional values and the teacher: a summary of key points

_____ *Being clear about expectations forms an important part of determining codes of behaviour for professionals.*

_____ *Expectations of teachers expressed by teachers, students and others may be at variance -- in clarifying expectations it is therefore important to know to whom an expectation belongs.*

_____ *Expectations of teachers form the basis for setting professional values for teachers.*

_____ *Text and drawings form the basis of two important classes of research tools for clarifying values.*

_____ *Beginning teachers must understand their own expectations of what it means to be a teacher in order to begin to build their own value set.*

_____ *Meeting the requirements for QTS means that a beginning teacher must be able to demonstrate behaviour consistent with the Standards in Section 1 of 'Qualifying to Teach'.*

_____ *Beginning teachers must build a value set which is consistent with the Standards and which is based on a thorough understanding of the role and expectations of a teacher as expressed by all of the stakeholders in education.*

Further reading

GTCE Professional Code for Teachers (available from **www.gtce.org.uk/gtcinfo/code.asp**). The Standards make reference to this Professional Code – it is obviously in the interests of all beginning teachers to have read this document and ensured that they have understood it.

General Medical Council Standards of Practice (available from **www.gmc-uk.org/standards/**) and The Guide to the Professional Conduct of Solicitors (available from **www.guide-on-line.lawsociety.org.uk/**). These two professional codes for doctors and lawyers provide an interesting comparison with the GTCE code. The code for doctors is relatively brief, while that for lawyers contains a great deal of information. Comparison of the three codes where common issues exist (for example, confidentiality) is a useful exercise for beginning teachers to conduct.

Koehn, D. (1994) *The Ground of Professional Ethics*. London. Routledge. For anyone wishing to consider professional ethics in more depth, this book provides a good starting point – although it is not for the faint-hearted! Teachers reading this book will find much of interest, although (as Haydon 1996 notes) they will find it necessary to infer what Koehn's arguments mean for teachers, since she refers to teaching only briefly, when discussing practices that might be considered as a profession.

For further information on professional values and the teacher, visit **www.learning matters.co.uk/education/learnteach/chapt1.html**

2 LEARNING AND LEARNING STYLES

GARY D. KINCHIN

Professional Standards for QTS

 2.1, 2.4, 3.1.1, 3.3.3

To be awarded QTS, you must know the content of the subject you are trained to teach. You should understand what can affect the learning of students in your classes. You must be able to set appropriate teaching and learning objectives based upon your knowledge of the students. You should teach lessons that employ interactive teaching and group work approaches and encourage active and independent learning where students take greater ownership of their learning.

You may find it helpful to read through the appropriate section of the handbook, which accompanies the Standards for the Award of QTS for clarification and support.

Introduction

As a soon-to-be-qualified teacher or new member of the profession, you are central to further raising standards within the education system (e.g. improvements in literacy and numeracy, greater numbers of students achieving five or more GCSEs at C or above), which were outlined in the White Paper – *Schools Achieving Success* (DfES 2001). The contributors to this book hope you agree that all teachers have a responsibility to know their subject and present the content in ways which enable students to learn (Bleach 2000). How learning occurs is clearly of importance for everyone working in classrooms, as students learning what was intended has been identified by some as the basis for describing effective teaching (e.g. Capel, Leask and Turner 1995, Kyriacou 1997).

While student learning should be your first consideration in planning and teaching, it is well documented that trainees and early career teachers possess only the beginnings of a knowledge base to achieve this objective and at the same time are more concerned with:

- **how they are going to cope with their workload and survive in the teaching environment;**
- **their classroom management and being regarded as a 'real teacher';**
- **being liked and accepted by students (Behets 1990, Fuller 1969, Kyriacou and Stephens 1999, Monk 2001).**

These may indeed be anxieties that you have felt.

Whereas the above concerns may not foreground learning or make direct reference to the different ways in which students learn, the promotion of learning will always remain one of the things that teachers are concerned about across their careers. Teaching is more enjoyable and satisfying when students are enthusiastically engaged in their learning and you feel they are involved in the content of the lesson!

Assuming that you are at the initial stages of understanding the nature of learning, learning theories, and how students might prefer to learn, the purpose of this chapter is fourfold.

1. To get you thinking about learning, what it is, and how you might consider it in one classroom and promote it in yours.
2. To provide a description of some of the learning styles which might exist within classrooms.
3. To consider some implications of the new Standards for the Award of Qualified Teacher Status (QTS) for enabling student learning.
4. To offer a brief summary of some current research which has particular implications for promoting student learning.

What is learning?

This is a difficult question to answer. Theorists do not all agree what learning is and how it occurs. Learning is a broad concept and perspectives on how learning takes place have been put forward by psychologists, linguists, neuroscientists and philosophers. There is clear agreement that learning is important. Gredler (2001) has provided some pertinent reasons why the ability to learn is so crucial.

1. Learning is important to the individual.
2. Learning develops competencies in a variety of school subjects in both childhood and adolescence.
3. Learning aids the acquisition of a variety of perspectives, values, and ways to interact with one another.
4. Learning enables an individual to adapt to a diverse lifestyle.
5. Learning develops the capacity for lifelong learning.
6. Learning helps to preserve cultural values and traditions.
7. Learning aids new discoveries and inventions.

The word learning would also seem to imply 'change'. Stevenson and Palmer (1994) argue that while learning might occur implicitly (without the individual being aware of it) or explicitly (where there is conscious and deliberate effort), most definitions suggest that learning is an enduring change in an individual as a consequence of an experience in a particular situation (Driscoll 1994). This however would seem to exclude changes which occur due to maturation/growth and development (Long 2000).

As you begin your career in teaching, Kyriacou (1997) perhaps offers one of the most helpful definitions of learning stating, 'pupil learning can be defined as changes in a pupil's behaviours which take place as a result of being engaged in an educational experience' (p.22). The changes implied here can span some of the many outcomes possible within a secondary school curriculum, as the following illustrate: greater knowledge of dates in history, having different attitudes towards certain issues or ideas in contexts of personal, social, and health education, the improved ability to play a musical instrument, demonstrating an understanding of photosynthesis in science through a group presentation, knowing all the major cities in France, or the application of a particular defensive strategy in an invasion game in physical education.

Learning here therefore suggests the capacity to do something different to what could be done earlier (Schunk 1996). Learning can also be described as a 'change of mind'.

UNDERSTANDING LEARNING: ONE VIEW FROM INSIDE THE CLASSROOM

In an effort to understand learning it is also important to understand the dynamics of classroom life. You and your students will spend considerable time in each other's presence. Creating teaching environments that are both orderly (which we know you are concerned about) and which promote learning will be difficult professional work. Your role as a teacher is to enable learning, which could suggest the direction of influence in class is solely from you to the student in terms of influencing their learning gains. In the dynamics of classroom life this is not always the case, and you may have experienced this. Students often exert great influence. For example, there may have been times when what is completed and hopefully learnt by students feels almost 'negotiated' between you and them, and that they are exploring the boundaries.

Not only are you faced with varying needs and learning styles but also varying levels of motivation to be in class and to learn. Being with friends and fulfilling their own agenda for social interaction (which you may regard as disruptive) may already have competed with your efforts to engage students with the content. Such a situation can impact on learning in the classroom as an explanation of the following 'model' indicates.

Doyle (1979, 1981) viewed the classroom as an 'ecology'. A brief insight into his model will provide one way of understanding the daily realities of classroom life and the challenges this poses for thinking about and enabling teaching and learning. Doyle saw the management, instructional and student social systems of the class interacting and developing around a series of tasks to be completed by students. If the ecological balance between these systems was right *in the eyes of students* then the instructional element is normally foregrounded and learning tasks and gains become priority. If not, then students may tend to fix the balance in their own way to make the tasks or work they are doing something they can achieve and enjoy, or they may go off-task and do something else which requires you to re-establish order and control.

Of relevance to some of the content of this chapter (in particular, sections where you are asked to consider some learning theories), Siedentop and Tannehill (2000) indicate that good teachers tend to be able to promote learning gains by blending the student social system into the instructional system by:

- **offering an exciting and relevant curriculum;**
- **employing strategies such as group work, which demand student interaction;**
- **promoting peer teaching and co-operative learning.**

It is therefore important to develop students' positive attitudes toward learning. The use of the above suggestions, while acknowledging how Doyle views the classroom, may be one way to see and appreciate the complexities of classroom life.

Theories of learning

As a new teacher, do you have your own personal theory or theories of how learning best takes place? Most teachers do, so it is possible that you do too. You are a learner yourself and have spent many hours observing teachers teaching you in their efforts to enable your learning.

Practical task

As you ponder your own personal theory of learning, consider some of the following questions.

- *What did you learn in and out of school?*
- *How did you learn these things?*
- *Under what circumstances did you learn best?*
- *What circumstances or arrangements tended to impede your learning?*
- *How might you use your own experiences as a learner to inform your efforts to enable learning in the classroom?*

Your responses to the above task might suggest your learning occurred differently for different tasks (some that were simple, some that were more complex). There may have been things that you learned either in the absence of a teacher (e.g. being with your classmates) or that could only have been learned *with* a teacher present. You might have recalled examples when class discussions and group work with others helped your learning or when you were required to recite facts successfully from memory alone.

Every intentional teaching/learning experience is built on assumptions about how learning happens, whether this is implicit or explicit (Rink 2001). When these assumptions about learning are formalised or abstracted to a more general level, we call them learning theories. According to Driscoll (1994) a learning theory represents 'a set of constructs linking observed changes in performance with what is thought to bring about those changes' (p. 9). In essence, learning theories have attempted to understand how individuals relate to their environment in ways that enhance their ability to use themselves and their environments more efficiently and more effectively.

As you may be aware, writers have put forward a vast number of theories in an effort to explain or describe how learning occurs. Not all theories, however, are applicable to those who work in education, but there are some that appear more dominant and have received greater attention in the literature. Child (1986) reminds us that 'no one theory has provided all the answers to the kinds of questions of concern to teachers … no one single theory has yet been formulated which satisfactorily accounts for all the facts' (p. 82).

The following section sets out the main premise of some of the positions/theories of learning. These theories may suit teachers but are not intended to polarise. The difference between the perspectives involves different ways of focusing on learning but both provide important insights into the processes of effective performance and learning. As Phillips and Soltis (1998) state: 'we must be content to deal with a number of theories of learning, each useful perhaps in a different context' (p. 5). Roblyer (1996) also reminds us, and the following section will attest, that there are opposing views as to whether learning should be structured and directed by teachers or taken charge of by students constructing their own knowledge and, in essence, having more ownership of that learning. Again, the situation will dictate. In summary, learning theories can be helpful to you in the following ways.

- **They can inform your planning and teaching.**
- **They can help you to evaluate your practice.**
- **They can assist in the diagnosis of in-class problems.**

Some theories of learning

All twentieth-century learning theories can be classified into two broad families: conditioning theories (behaviourist family), and interactionist theories (cognitive family). There are differences between these two families: the behaviourist position, that humans are passive beings and therefore react to stimuli; and the cognitive position, that learners are interactive. However, no learning theory can ignore the critical nature of the level of student engagement or that motivation is a key factor influencing whether learning does or does not take place. High achievement in learning is more likely when the student is highly motivated as motivation represents a key factor influencing the extent to which students can achieve desirable learning outcomes.

We shall examine perspectives on learning promulgated by theorists within the behaviourist and cognitive families, which some claim to have had the most significant impact upon learning and teaching within schools (Child 1986).

Behaviourist family

If as a teacher on placement you have used immediate praise and positive feedback to students as examples of positive reinforcement, or have applied consequences for inappropriate behaviour such as detentions, or you have taught and re-taught with feedback how you want your students to enter and exit the classroom then you have already incorporated aspects of Skinnerian theory in your teaching. If you are looking to further use Skinner's ideas then you will be predominantly concerned with finding ways to get your learners to respond and then reinforce that response. The resultant behaviour should subsequently be reinforced for it is more likely to occur again under similar circumstances.

SKINNER

B. F. Skinner (1968), as the founder of operant conditioning, is considered by some to be the most influential theorist to have an impact on education and learning. Advocates of behaviourism view learning as a permanent transformation in behaviour with an emphasis upon measurable changes or outcomes. Learning is seen as a conditioning process concerned with a response to a stimulus. The stimulus is deemed the cause of learning which acts upon the individual evoking the response or increasing the chances of a response. In the absence of this reinforcement, the behaviour is less likely to occur. Learning is therefore interpreted in terms of the strength of the stimulus-response connection. Behaviourists suggest teachers should therefore:

- **create environments that enable students to respond properly to stimuli;**
- **be specific about what are appropriate responses;**
- **model good behaviour;**
- **shape appropriate behaviour by rewarding positive responses.**

Cognitive family

In your teaching to date, you may have:

- **provided opportunities for your students to learn in problem-solving settings;**
- **included content that students are passionate about (that is, you see the importance of making the learning experiences relevant and meaningful for your students with an awareness of the students' current knowledge);**
- **used teaching which concentrated on the unknown using the known as a basis.**

If so, then not only have you seen elements of Doyle's thinking on a practical level, but you have already begun to incorporate aspects of cognitive learning theory in your teaching, as the following will explain.

Cognitive theorists have attended to more holistic perspectives on learning with specific interest in the ways learners solve problems. Vygotsky (1962) and Bruner (1966) are considered some of the most influential theorists within this family. According to Bruner (1966), the acquisition of knowledge is an active process. Individuals construct knowledge by connecting the incoming facts to previously acquired knowledge. It is here that the individuals make meaning.

Cognitive theorists typically place action and problem-solving at the centre of learning. Learning is viewed as a process of gaining or changing insights, views, or outlooks as individuals make meaning of previously learned facts. Learning is inferred from what people say or do. Thus, the learning process is primarily social and learning occurs through socialisation carried out in a variety of contexts, such as the school, the family, or peer group. (You will recall that in Doyle's model there was a very heavy emphasis upon the social task system and how teachers might develop this to achieve instructional objectives.) The assumption here is that students will learn when placed in these groups, or other interactive settings, as much of what is learned is learned from others (Vygotsky, 1962).

CONSTRUCTIVISM
According to Marlowe and Page (1998),

> ... passively accumulating disconnected knowledge is not learning ... To learn a student has to be mentally and often physically active. A student learns when she discovers her own answers, solutions, concepts and relationships and creates her own interpretations (p. 12).

The above statement offers one rationale for constructivism as a school of thought on learning. Of late, constructivism and situated learning have become quite popular orientations to teaching and learning as a part of the cognitive family (Rink 2001). The constructivist approach has had a significant impact upon instruction and learning (Capel, Leask and Turner 1997, Kyriacou 1997), and is viewed by some as a component within the cognitive sciences (Terwel 1999) and as a theory about how we learn (Marlowe and Page 1998). Constructivist approaches support the position that learners are not passive recipients of transmitted knowledge. Constructivism emphasises the active role students play in acquiring knowledge personally and socially through engagement with meaningful tasks situated within their immediate environment. Rather than being given specific information on how the task is to be performed, constructivist approaches encourage learners to find their own way through the tasks, developing and creating their own knowledge. Learner autonomy and initiative is accepted and encouraged and knowledge is created by doing, researching and experiencing real-life situations (Roelofs and Terwel 1999). In effect, as the term suggests, learners attempt to 'construct' individual meanings based upon what they currently understand and know. Constructivism assumes that all learners have had different experiences therefore individual understanding cannot be the same between people.

Constructivist approaches foreground the knowledge structures students currently possess, which is termed 'conceptions' within the educational literature. Research that originates in cognitive psychology provides considerable support for the presence of students' prior knowledge: that is, students come to every new learning experience with some knowledge about the topic already established (Dodds, Griffin and Placek 2001). For learning to take place the student must understand the new material in terms of their existing prior knowledge (Taber 2001). There is a growing literature across a number of the subjects including science, maths, PE, health, geography and history on students' conceptions – that is, what they know and believe about a topic (see Barratt and Hacking 2000, Galili and Bar 1997, Griffin, Dodds, Placek and Tremino 2001, Myhill 2000, Pendry, Atha, Carden, Courtney, Keogh and Ruston 1997, Placek, Griffin, Dodds, Raymond, Tremino and James 2001). These conceptions have been labelled preconceptions, misconceptions, alternative conceptions or alternative frameworks. An understanding of alternative conceptions is critical if genuine learning is to occur (Palmer 2001), as it is quite common for learners to enter classrooms with ideas related to topics, which are at odds with expert opinion or viewpoints (Taber 2001).

Practical task

You are planning to teach a lesson in your subject area. During the closure of the preceding lesson introduce the next topic(s):

- *ask the students to write down what they currently know or believe regarding the topic and what they consider to be some of the sources of their present knowledge.*

Collect the written task. Before you read the responses:

- *predict and write down what you expect your students to possess some prior knowledge of in relation to the topic(s);*
- *list what might be some possible sources of this knowledge.*

Read the responses and attempt to collate them.

- *Compare and contrast your predictions with the present knowledge and sources of knowledge among the students – what emerged?*
- *How did the nature of their knowledge compare with your conceptions of the topic that you are about to teach?*
- *What are the implications of these findings for enabling learning in your subject?*

Marlowe and Page (1998) offer some implications for work in classrooms if teachers wish to adopt the constructivist perspective.

- **Teachers should emphasise the promotion of learning via questioning and problem solving.**
- **Teachers should de-emphasise the transmission of knowledge.**
- **Work in the classroom should retain the importance of the content to be unearthed and reflected upon.**
- **Individuals' conceptions of the content are foregrounded to help learners decide between the relevant/meaningful and the irrelevant.**

In summary:

1. Learners construct knowledge actively and socially.
2. Learners already possess ideas about the learning situation.
3. Learners take greater responsibility for and ownership of their learning.

If you take account of what you currently do in your teaching and consider some of your most recent experiences with your classes, it may be quite possible that you have used some activities/tasks which illustrate the above positions on learning. If you can associate yourself with some of the activities below then you could well have incorporated some elements of them in your classrooms already. Have you:

- **asked your students in their groups to predict the outcome of a science experiment before they begin?**
- **used punishment to discourage certain types of activities?**
- **developed an interactive multi-media presentation to make a topic more interesting in geography?**
- **asked students to count to 50 in French and then praised them for this?**
- **allowed the students in your class to set their own personal targets in physical education when fulfilling a role of their choice (e.g. team leader)?**
- **structured an environment in a citizenship session where your students engaged in critical thinking?**
- **used a reward to encourage your students to complete a task in history?**

- played background music to encourage a mood or stimulate a group routine within dance?
- provided your students with the materials to create their own presentations in IT?

On the surface you may not realise that the fundamental underpinnings throughout these tasks are quite different, but part of becoming an effective teacher will be your ability to quite skilfully blend these different approaches and positions on learning for different classroom-based situations.

LEARNING STYLES

Research and writing on learning styles has attended to efforts to define learning styles, and has documented elaborate attempts to understand and categorise elements that make up different learning styles. While writers have put forward multiple definitions, (Cano-Garcia and Hughes 2001), throughout educational research the idea of 'learning style' typically refers to how people prefer to learn (Heffler 2001, Kolb 1984, Sternberg 1997) and thus access and process ideas and new information.

You may have been informed as part of your training or induction that one reason why learning may not take place is a possible mismatch between students' preferred learning style and the learning opportunities and tasks they face. There is general agreement that individuals do indeed differ in their preferences for gathering and processing information. Like adults, children and students do learn in different ways. Felder and Silverman (1988) and Barbe and Malone (1981) claim students and young people could be considered hear-learners, see-learners or do-learners. Individuals will rely upon a consistent set of behaviours or approaches to learning and seeking meaning (Van Zwanenberg, Wilkinson and Anderson 2000) which are determined by a combination of hereditary, environmental factors, and the demands of the present environment.

Research on teaching to different learning styles is not conclusive with reference to the impact upon students' academic achievement (Muijs and Reynolds 2001). However, a number of writers have attempted to 'catalogue' a range of learning styles that exist across individuals or have produced inventories to enable learners to self-report their preferences. An extensive review of this literature is not appropriate here. The reader is encouraged to consult Riding and Raynor (1998) and Honey and Mumford (1982). For the purposes of this chapter the work of Kolb (1976, 1984, 1985), and Honey and Mumford (1982) will be discussed followed by some attention to Gardener's theory of Multiple Intelligences.

Kolb: Learning Styles Inventory (LSI)

One of the most noted writers in the area of learning styles is Kolb. Kolb's LSI is arguably the most widely documented instrument for measuring and analysing learning styles (Kolb 1984). Kolb (1976) identified four adaptive learning modes, which are summarised in Table 1.

Learning mode	Unique characteristics
Concrete experience	Responds to kinaesthetic elements of the experience
Reflective observation	Learns by introspection and reflection
Abstract concept	Comprehends information conceptually
Active experimentation	Learns by environmental manipulation

Table I: Summary of Kolb's learning modes and associated characteristics.

The construct of learning style as identified by Kolb included two dimensions. Firstly, perceiving, which describes the concrete and abstract thinker, and secondly, processing, which describes the active or reflective processing ability. When these dimensions were integrated by Kolb some alternative ways of relating to the world were expressed as four types of learning styles.

1. Divergers: who learn by personal experience gathered from feelings.
2. Assimilators: experience is grasped through abstract comprehension.
3. Convergers: use abstract reflection.
4. Accommodators: process information concretely and actively.

Kolb (1984) offered a conceptualisation of learning through the 'experiential learning cycle'. This model described learning as a continuous cyclical process of experience, reflection, theory and preparation. The ability to learn, according to Kolb, can commence at any point in the cycle. The individual elements of the sequence are described as follows:

- *Experience*: represents an active experience where new information is fed in.
- *Reflection*: process of learning change, the individual now passively thinks about what has just happened.
- *Theory*: the individual thinks about the new information and now contrasts this with other ideas and theories.
- *Preparation*: this is where the learner considers what to do next.

Honey and Mumford

Honey and Mumford (1982) applied Kolb's experiential cycle to produce a learning styles model that consisted of four descriptions of individuals who prefer to learn at the respective stages of the Kolb cycle. Their 20-item questionnaire enables the individual to locate their preferred learning style. Cotton (1995) offers a useful summary of the characteristics of each learning style, which has been outlined in Table 2.

Style	Stage of Kolb's experiential learning cycle	Characteristics
Active learners	Experience	Welcomes new experiences, rushes into new experiences, takes centre stage, easily bored, happy to combine with others, likes opportunities for problem solving. **Activists** are individuals who learn by doing, enjoy novel experiences, and generally dislike structured situations
Reflective learners	Reflection	Are cautious, tend to take a back seat, are calm, prefer to take their time, generally have a low profile and are more disposed to observational experiences. **Reflectors** are individuals who learn through feelings and experience, enjoy asking questions and try to predict outcomes
Theorists	Theory	Learn by investigation, carry out tasks in logical steps, and think through application of general rules. **Theorists** are individuals who learn through observation and investigation and tend to focus upon logic and systematic planning
Pragmatists	Preparation	Tend to try out ideas in practice, they want to get on with things, and thrive on direct work experience. **Pragmatists** are individuals who learn by thinking and engaging in problem-solving and role-playing

Table 2: Summary of Honey and Mumford's learning styles with associated characteristics.

Multiple intelligences

GARDNER

As we have seen, many learning styles can be found within one classroom. The intellectual strengths and weaknesses each student possesses will determine how easy or difficult it is for this individual to learn the content presented in a particular way by the teacher. As an attempt to recognise the different abilities and talents of students, Howard Gardner (1983) proposed a new concept of intelligence and formulated a list of seven intelligences.

1. Logical-mathematical intelligence: logical thinking, deductive reasoning (mathematical and scientific thinking).
2. Linguistic intelligence: mastery of language to remember information.
3. Spatial intelligence: development of mental images to solve problems.
4. Musical intelligence: recognition of musical tones, pitches and rhythms.

5. Bodily-kinesthetic intelligence: mental ability is used to co-ordinate bodily movement.

6. Personal intelligences: includes interpersonal feelings of others and intrapersonal intelligence which is the ability to understand one's own feelings and motives.

Gardner claimed the intelligences are needed for productive functioning in our society, that they rarely operate alone, but are used concurrently when facing problems or acquiring skills.

Gardener suggests some implications for teachers, as follows.

- **Think of all the intelligences as equally important.**
- **Present material that attends to most, if not all, the intelligences.**
- **Use knowledge of the intelligences to reinforce the content in multiple ways.**
- **Implement different assessment techniques to enable learners to show what they know, understand and can do (journals, portfolios, creative tasks).**

Guidance on teaching for multiple intelligences is available; see, for example, Jasmine (1996).

Practical task

During the induction phase of your placement in a secondary school, you will undoubtedly observe lessons taught by your mentor and other experienced teachers. Take the opportunity during these observation periods to focus on the students and their learning.

Focus on:
- *what the students are asked to do;*
- *how the students approach what they are asked to do;*
- *how the students respond to opportunities to work independently and to make their own decisions.*

More specifically focus on the following areas:
- *Identify three students in a class or across a number of different classes whose lessons you are going to observe over a short period, preferably classes that you will eventually teach yourself.*
- *During the lessons, focus on these students and make some brief notes about how they engage in the lesson, how they respond to the tasks or activities, how they relate to other students and the teacher, any apparent 'misconceptions' or misunderstandings and the quality of their 'products' or lesson outcomes.*
- *As the students work, talk to them about what they are doing and how they are approaching the task. A question that asks them whether they are finding the work easy or difficult would be a useful starting point.*
- *Are you able to come to any conclusion about these students and their 'preferred learning styles'?*
- *Talk to your mentor or the class teacher about your observations.*
- *Try to use the information you have gathered in this task in your planning for these groups and students.*

As a new teacher do you sense that some of your students might prefer structure, or that some might prefer learning on their own? Are there some students who seem to prefer situations when the room is silent? Do you recognise these seven intelligences within the classes you teach?

Catering for such an array of needs will be a challenging task for trainees and newly qualified teachers when interacting with large groups of learners. In order to progress towards meeting the Standards for the Award of Qualified Teacher Status (QTS) it is important that beginning teachers are aware of the different learning styles that might exist in their classes and what might be some characteristics of individual learning styles. Such information will influence how you organise the curriculum, select appropriate teaching strategies and their accompanying learning experiences or tasks to enable access to the content for all students.

The QTS Standards: implications for student learning

How do the new professional Standards impact on trainees to enable student learning? In this section, attention is drawn to some aspects of the Standards that appear most relevant for enabling learning.

The Standards make reference to the need to 'employ interactive teaching methods and collaborative group work ... promote active and independent learning' (QTS 3.3.3). Mention was made earlier of the typical concerns/fears most inexperienced teachers feel during the very early stages of their development and training. These could limit the range of teaching approaches that are adopted. Newly qualified teachers will also experience a range of stressors during a period which Katz (1972) referred to as 'survival' and which is a time when teachers are coping on a daily basis, and may be questioning their ability to teach. Acknowledging Fuller's three-stage model of teacher development (Fuller 1969), moving from (a) concerns about self, to (b) concerns about tasks, to (c) concerns about students and the impact of teaching, seems pertinent here and leads us to ask whether trainee teachers are capable of achieving such a focus upon outcome rather than on self so early in their development as teachers.

It has been documented that inexperienced teachers tend to adopt more direct forms of instruction that both lead to less developed independent learning skills among students (Gipps and McGilchrist 1999) and does not 'connect material' (Muijs and Reynolds 2001, p. 15). Indeed in some subject areas Ofsted (1995) have highlighted that experienced teachers have tended to use more command styles of instruction. If this is the case with veteran teachers, can we expect trainees to have sufficient pedagogical knowledge to provide, monitor, and manage learner-centred environments (couched within cognitive/constructivist schools of thought) when they are typically 'getting to grips' with subject and curricular knowledge?

If we aim to develop the very best teachers then the answer to the above question has to be yes. However, all of us involved in initial teacher education realise the difficulty and complexity inherent in this process, and one of the primary functions of any teacher education programme has to be the provision of support in the achievement of this goal. It seems timely to heed Kyriacou and Stephen's (1999) remark in their study of PGCE students:

> If student teachers believe that students should be occupied principally to keep bad behaviour at bay, future generations of teachers are going to be more preoccupied with the management of 'order' than the cultivation of learning (p. 28).

Learning and learning styles:
a summary of key points

___ **Student learning should be the first consideration in teaching a lesson.**

___ **Learning theories typically fall within one of two categories (behaviourist and cognitive).**

___ **Learning styles refer to how individuals prefer to learn. Several learning styles and their associated characteristics have been identified by researchers (Kolb, Honey and Mumford) and show that individuals operate various 'intelligences' differentially (see Gardner).**

___ **Individuals with different learning styles possess some unique characteristics.**

___ **Constructivism represents a dominant school of thought on learning. An understanding of students' prior conceptions is critical in helping them connect new learning with established knowledge structures.**

Further reading

Gardner, H. (1983) *Frames of Mind: The Theory of Multiple Intelligences*. New York. Basic Books Inc. An examination of the theory of Multiple Intelligences framed within the notion that all humans possess at least seven different competencies. Gardner describes the characteristics associated with each of these intelligences and how they operate in varying degrees depending upon each person's individual profile.

Wood, D. (1998) *How Children Think and Learn* (2nd ed.). Oxford. Blackwell. Informed by cognitive theory this book outlines how thinking and learning in children are positioned within social contexts. How language is acquired and what factors tend to impede progress are examined. Considerable attention is afforded to the implications of cognitive research and how this research transfers to the teacher's world of work.

For further information on learning and learning styles, visit **www.learningmatters. co.uk/education/learnteach/chapt2.html**

Professional Standards for QTS

 1.7, 2.2, 3.1.1, 3.1.2, 3.1.4, 3.2.4, 3.3.3, 3.3.7, 3.3.8, 3.3.12

To be awarded QTS you must have high expectations of your students. You need to demonstrate that you carefully evaluate your own work so that your contribution to raising students' educational attainments is as effective as possible. You must be aware of the general teaching requirements of the National Curriculum and be able to plan lessons and sequences of lessons in your specialist subject that are related to particular students' abilities and interests and the expected standards for their age. Your planning may involve the deployment of additional adults to support students' learning as part of your differentiation of work for students. Your students will understand what it is you want them to learn and why, and your skills of time and resource management will support the learning process.

You may find it helpful to read through the appropriate section of the handbook which accompanies the Standards for the Award of QTS for clarification and support.

Introduction

This chapter addresses the key issues of teacher preparation and planning for learning. It follows on from the themes of Chapter 2, with its overview of theories of learning and cognition, and anticipates those of Chapter 4, a chapter concerned with the vitally important and inseparable issue of assessment of – and *for* – learning. Underlying this chapter as a whole is the assumption that the processes of teaching and learning are inextricably bound up with questions of knowledge, that teachers and students are dealing with what is often referred to as 'content' and that – in the UK context – this is often specified by the National Curriculum, National Strategies or examination syllabuses. Herbert Kohl, whilst stressing the importance of the interpersonal dimension of teaching as an activity – responding to students' preferred learning styles and contributing positively to the development of learners' identities – put it like this:

> Teaching does not consist *solely* of making youngsters feel good about themselves. It involves helping students acquire understanding, knowledge, and skills they didn't previously have. To do this, it is essential to enable students to feel good about themselves as learners and to create an atmosphere that enables them to focus energy on learning. But this is not all there is to teaching well. Thought has to be given to the content of what is to be learned and to the way this content is presented.
>
> (Kohl 1986, p. 90, my italics)

More recently, writing about major reform of the school system in the Australian state of Queensland, Allan Luke identified three areas of intervention that can 'make a difference' to students 'at risk': social support; basic skills and direct instruction; and intellectual engagement. Luke's point is that it is intellectual engagement and depth that is the key:

... where there is social support and help with skills, intellectual engagement may be necessary and sufficient to 'bootstrap' up the achievement of our most at risk students. (Luke 1999, p. 12)

CURRICULUM AND LEARNING

The word 'curriculum' comes from the Latin word *currere* (to run) and means a course of study (to be run) or a set of ideas (to be taught and developed). In England and Wales, the first ever National Curriculum was implemented in 1989 (Scotland and Northern Ireland have never had a National Curriculum). This was the first time that a range of subject knowledge, understanding and skills had been specified across the 5 to 16 age-range. The National Curriculum became a statutory instrument and its implementation has been monitored ever since through the inspection system. These new arrangements supplemented the syllabuses for 16+ and 18+ national examinations with which secondary teachers have worked for a very long time. Since September 2001, secondary schools have also been asked to work with the Key Stage 3 National Strategy. This non-statutory but recommended initiative has been designed to address the difficulties many students experience on transition from the primary phase in accessing the secondary curriculum and also the problem of student regression (in terms of attainment) between Key Stage 2 and the early years of Key Stage 3.

Practical task

In your school (and preferably in your own subject department), find a teacher who was teaching prior to the introduction of the National Curriculum in 1989. How did this teacher design a course of study – a curriculum – for students then? What are the differences now? What are the benefits and drawbacks (for individual students, teachers and society) of a National Curriculum?

The activity of teacher planning, then, has become more complex over the last 13 years as more detailed curriculum prescription in terms of 'subject matter' – combined with a more recent emphasis on recommended teaching methods and strategies – means that individual teachers (through their work in subject departments) have had to 'map' their curriculum against national frameworks as well as examination syllabuses. This complexity arises from the obvious requirement to consider the children to be taught first (their needs, interests and preferred learning styles), the available resources (physical, including the classroom, sports equipment, textbooks, musical instruments, computers, library stock, etc; and human, including classroom assistants and teacher expertise) and the students' entitlement to the National Curriculum, Key Stage 3 National Strategy and what is generally referred to as the ideal of a 'broad and balanced curriculum'. Complex planning at this level is discussed later in this chapter but, as a trainee, you will need to be aware of how your work – and that of your department – relates to the rest of a student's experience of the secondary curriculum.

DIFFERENT TRADITIONS IN PLANNING FOR LEARNING: A SUMMARY

One of the most influential models of teacher planning and preparation was that of Tyler (1949). Tyler's original theories of instructional design were based on behaviourist approaches to learning. The psychologist Jerome Bruner (1966) expounded theories of teaching and learning that were focused on the processes of mental growth and the teacher's role in facilitating this. Glaser (1976, 1984) later critiqued what he saw as 'process-based' approaches to instruction but proposed a 'knowledge-based' or 'competency' model that to some extent reflected Bruner's notion of 'optimal structures' of knowledge:

> … a theory of instruction must specify the ways in which a body of knowledge should be structured so that it can be most readily grasped by the learner. 'Optimal structure' refers to a set of propositions from which a larger body of knowledge can be generated … since the merit of a structure depends upon its power for *simplifying information*, for *generating new propositions*, and for *increasing the manipulability of a body of knowledge*, structure must always be related to the status and gifts of the learner. Viewed in this way, the optimal structure of a body of knowledge is not absolute but relative.
>
> (Bruner 1966, p. 4I; emphasis in original)

Shulman (1986) outlined various domains of knowledge and their relationship to effective teaching and learning and suggested that the role of subject knowledge in teacher development was under-researched but vitally important. Recent inspection evidence from Ofsted (2002) suggests that effective departments in secondary schools do not necessarily have more detailed or thorough schemes of work but that what exists clearly specifies what knowledge, skills and understanding should be covered with a class and how students can make progress.

For many beginning teachers, this is one of the most difficult aspects of planning. How do you represent ideas or model skills that you have developed at the graduate level to, say, a bottom set Year 9 last thing on a Friday afternoon during a force eight gale? The Standards for the Award of QTS – and this book – assume that much of your training will concern the principles of developing 'optimal structures' in your own specialist subject and providing you with opportunities to practise this in classrooms.

THE QUESTION OF TEACHER KNOWLEDGE

> He who can, does.
> He who cannot, teaches.   (George Bernard Shaw)

As we stated at the opening of the chapter, a teacher teaches children *something*. The Standards for the Award of QTS specify that you should understand the subject knowledge requirements of your own specialist subject. The development of your subject knowledge in the context of the secondary classroom is outside the remit of this book but will be an important part of your training. Contrary to Shaw's famous aphorism, however, teachers need to be able to know and do; they must also understand what they are doing and what they know. It is the ability to understand and make explicit that understanding that distinguishes a good teacher.

When discussing teaching strategies, Kohl draws attention to the importance of the teacher's knowledge of the subject:

> There are many other modes of explanation, such as drawing diagrams, providing examples, or even improvising a dramatic presentation of an idea. All these

techniques require a mastery of the content you are teaching so that you are free to play with it.

(Kohl 1986, p. 102)

In other words, in order to teach effectively, matching content and method to the particular children's needs – and to analyse what the children have learned – teachers need to be able to be able to reshape ideas, to represent knowledge in different ways. This is only possible if teachers have confidence in their own knowledge.

WAYS TO DEVELOP YOUR SUBJECT KNOWLEDGE

Subject knowledge is only one kind of teacher knowledge that Shulman (1986) identified as being important for effective teaching. Other domains of knowledge include knowledge of the children and how children learn, and knowledge of the classroom culture and the school. One aim of your training is to transform what you already know into pedagogical content knowledge, that is to say, subject knowledge that is available to you in the classroom for teaching. This is the process through which biology graduates transpose what they know about, for example, photosynthesis into lesson content for a Year 7 group. In addition, it will often be necessary for you to develop some aspects of subject knowledge that are new to you (for example, explicit knowledge of sentence grammar for some English specialists). There are many ways to develop new areas of subject knowledge that will also help to make what you already know 'pedagogically available' (useful and useable in teaching and learning). These include:

- **observation of experienced teachers;**
- **collaborative teaching with mentor or other experienced teachers;**
- **independent reading and study (of appropriate text books and classroom resources);**
- **workshops within a differentiated training programme.**

Planning for learning over time

Teaching is sometimes described as a cycle of:

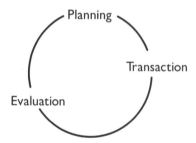

Figure 1: The teaching cycle.

Simply put:

- **planning goes on before teaching;**
- **transaction is what happens in the classroom with students;**
- **and evaluation occurs after teaching.**

However, the reality is more complex.

The planning stage includes a consideration of aims, justifications, subject knowledge and skills, strategies, assessment and resources. It is ongoing and plans are adjusted based on assessment information.

The transaction stage is the execution of the plans made earlier (although in practice the transaction may involve changes of plan in response to the emerging and unforeseeable responses of the learners). Simultaneous evaluation of the transaction can lead to changes in planning. Transaction – implying, as it does, interaction and interplay – is a term that is used in preference to *delivery*. Deliveries can be made whilst the intended recipients are 'out'.

The evaluation stage includes a comparison of the learner's achievements in the lesson with the teacher's plans; and an evaluation of the effectiveness of the teaching strategies and resources used. The evaluation is part of the planning stage for the next and subsequent teaching activities/lessons.

But why bother writing lesson plans?

It is worth stating explicitly here that your initial training's emphasis upon careful and thorough planning, and reflective, critical evaluation, is to ensure high standards of teaching and learning (the 'transaction') through which your students will make progress. Planning and evaluation are not simply administrative requirements. There are at least two main reasons why trainees are asked to plan carefully and thoroughly.

1. For new teachers without substantial classroom experience, the planning process is often difficult. In trying to plan teaching that is successful for you and your students and draws upon your own strengths (rather than simply trying to copy successful lessons you have observed), you will need to spend time thinking about what you want the students to learn and how they will achieve this. The very process of trying to write a plan – including the inevitable redrafting and revisions – will help you to develop planning skills. There is a body of research that views writing as a mode of learning (see, for example, Emig 1977) and so writing lesson plans can be seen as being useful to you, the trainee.

2. As a trainee, you will need to demonstrate – consistently and over a period of time – certain skills and attributes, including those contained within the QTS Standards. You will need to demonstrate your achievement of these Standards to a variety of people to whom you are accountable: your mentor and tutor, an external examiner and, perhaps, an inspector during an inspection of your training course or school. The evidential requirements for trainee teachers are sometimes seen as greater than for fully qualified teachers. This shouldn't be surprising. That said, qualified teachers seeking threshold payments or applying for Advanced Skills status (or indeed going through Ofsted inspection or post-Ofsted special measures) all have to produce detailed plans and records as part of portfolios of evidence.

Nevertheless, you will be aware that experienced teachers do not appear to 'need to plan' as much as you do. This doesn't mean that experienced teachers' plans aren't as detailed as yours; rather that 'experienced teachers more often rely on their extensive experience to form a mental framework of how they want the lesson to proceed' and that their plans 'have become internalised through repetition' (Kyriacou 1991, p. 17).

Long-term planning: schemes of work or key stage plans

A scheme of work is a description of the work planned for pupils over a specific period. Sometimes, they are known as key stage plans if they relate to the groupings of National Curriculum years. The planning of these is the responsibility of the whole subject department in a secondary school, co-ordinated by the head of department with all members of staff contributing to the planning process. It is at this level that the links between planning and teacher development become clear: different teachers with differing strengths contribute to the design of a curriculum for students in which teacher expertise is shared.

Long-term plans usually show less detail than shorter-term plans. At departmental level a scheme of work is made up from a series of units of work which describe:

- **how a school's curriculum policy is to be translated into effective teaching;**
- **how the curriculum will be implemented;**
- **how human and material resources will be used efficiently.**

To develop a scheme of work, departments will need to decide on an overall programme with regard to the range and depth of experiences/topics/activities they teach and ensure progression and continuity of student learning. The National Curriculum and the relevant national strategies and examination syllabuses will inform this process.

Practical task

Talk to your mentor about your subject department's approach to longer-term planning. How does the department go about planning at this level and reviewing their plans? What kinds of long-term planning records are kept?

The cover sheet to one department's key stage plan is reproduced opposite. It is not intended to be exemplary and we would need to see the detailed (medium-term) planning that followed it. It does, however, give us the opportunity to see how one secondary department (in this case, English) represents its Key Stage 3 programme on one side of A4.

Induction unit: making a student prospectus; – writing non-fiction	**Writing/telling autobiography** – differences between speech and writing	**Class novel study** *Tea Leaf on the Roof* by Jean Ure – language awareness – social variation
Extended simulation activity – Escape from Kraznir- – drama (role-play, writing in role, etc)	**Expressive arts project** – based on the *Beowulf* story – ICT Focus (multimedia)	**Diaries – integrated project** – Diary of a Survivor – pre-1914 non-fiction

Y7

. . . .

Individual poetry anthology
– writing poetry
– using quotation
	The language of advertising (media focus)
	– media
	– languages
	– audiences
		Drama text for class study
		– *Frankenstein-*
		  (inc. comparison with
		  Mary Shelley's novel)

Class novel study – choice of Anne Fine texts	**Individual/group extended narrative** – narrative POV	**Introduction to media studies** – media technologies

Y8

. . . .

Presenting a written argument
– response to non literary
  texts
– persuasion
	Forms of poetry
	– ballads and sonnets
		Class novel study
		– theme: different
		  generations – choice of
		  Robert Westall or Aiden
		  Chambers texts

Drama text as class study – Shakespeare	**Control of narrative**	**Newspapers** – their production and impact – ICT Focus

Y9

– independent reading programme

– literacy skills programme (KS3 starter activities and Literacy Progress Units where appropriate)

– ICT available – limited but systems in place for use

– information skills (Year 7)
– storytelling (Year 8)   cross-curricular projects
– newspaper (Year 9)

Figure I. Key Stage 3 plan for English.

Medium-term planning: units of work/sequences of lessons

These are the plans for the teaching of one of the components of the scheme of work, i.e. a topic, skill, text or activity, which will involve a series of lessons, perhaps over a five or six week period (one half of an average term). The planning of these is sometimes the responsibility of individual teachers, although departments often collaborate in this. In some cases, the unit of work is detailed to the level of content of individual lessons. As a beginning trainee, you will not normally be asked to design an entire unit of work from the start but, instead, you are likely to be given specific content and asked to plan an individual lesson. As you progress, however, you will be given increasing responsibility for designing your own units of work.

An effective medium-term plan shows how lessons fit together, indicates the progress expected and is a way of identifying targets for progression that apply to groups rather than individual students. An effective medium-term plan should:

- **identify what pupils will learn over a half-term/term;**
- **be based on assessments of what students already know, understand and can do;**
- **show evidence of progression, in line with the department's scheme of work or key stage plan; this may be in the form of differentiated expectations (see below);**
- **give recommendations for teaching and learning approaches;**
- **identify opportunities for assessment.**

An example of a medium-term plan (unit of work) proforma used by one training provider is shown in Figure 2. It is not presented as an example of good practice. As a guiding principle, we should recognise that different secondary, specialist subjects will have different planning requirements and that any generic proforma is meant to be adapted or used in the development of personalised planning formats. If you like, the boxes are not important; the thinking is.

You will notice that a good deal of information is required on this plan and that some of it will require considerable thought. Remember that some departments' units of work may not be as detailed but, in the context of your training, a proforma like this gives you the opportunity to demonstrate your understanding (briefly and meaningfully) of a number of key areas related to planning such as the cross-curricular learning specified at the beginning of each National Curriculum document and in the Key Stage 3 National Strategy.

LEARNING ACROSS THE CURRICULUM

All teachers have responsibility to develop their students' capacities in a number of areas. The National Curriculum specifies a number of general teaching requirements (including the use of language and ICT across the curriculum) and seven aspects of cross-curricular learning:

- **key skills;**
- **spiritual, moral, social and cultural development;**
- **thinking skills;**
- **work-related learning;**
- **education for sustainable development;**
- **enterprise and entrepreneurial skills;**
- **financial capability.**

Secondary QTS **Unit of work**	Year Group:	Date developed: Date revised:

Unit title: Focus:	The rationale for this unit:
Aims:	Potential outcomes for summative assessment purposes:
Particular resources:	Opportunities to develop cross-curricular dimensions:
	Links to previous work:
Health and safety issues:	Language for learning/KS3 Literacy objectives: KS3 Numeracy: KS3 ICT:

Learning across the curriculum: Key Skills:

Communication
Application of Number
ICT
Improving own learning and performance
Working with others
Problem solving

Other learning across the curriculum:
Contribution to Students' Spiritual, Moral, Social and Cultural development/ Thinking skills/Work-related learning/Education for sustainable development/Enterprise and entrepreneurial skills/Financial capability

Tasks/Activities	NC Programmes of Study/KS3 Strategy Objectives/A-Level AOs	Teaching approaches (including use of ICT)

Differentiated expectations:	AT and NC Level or exam criterion and grade, etc.:
1. After completing the unit, **most** students will have: 2. After completing the unit, **some** students will **not have made as much progress** and will: 3. After completing the unit, **some** students will **have progressed further** and will:	

Figure 2: Unit of work proforma.

For further information on key skills, see Chapter 9.

The Key Stage 3 strategies support the development of cross-curricular literacy, numeracy and the use of ICT. For further details, see Chapters 6, 7 and 8.

As an individual trainee, you shouldn't feel obliged to take full responsibility for all aspects of students' learning across the curriculum. This responsibility can only be assumed by the school and planned for collaboratively across departments and pastoral areas. You should, however, be interested if your specialist subject can make a contribution and be aware of how your own teaching might contribute. The sections on the unit of work proforma concerned with key skills and spiritual, moral, social and cultural development/other learning across the curriculum would only be completed if there were obvious ways in which the unit contributed to the development of students' capacities in these areas. For examples of how secondary subjects can contribute to these areas of cross-curricular learning, go to **www.nc. uk.net/ learn.html**

GENERAL TEACHING REQUIREMENTS: HEALTH AND SAFETY

One of the general teaching requirements specified by the National Curriculum is that of ensuring the health and safety of students. This requirement applies particularly to teachers of Design Technology, Art and Design, Physical Education, Science and ICT. Training in these specialist subjects will include attention to this important aspect of planning and teaching. On a medium-term plan, it is useful to draw attention to particular health and safety issues associated with the topic or activities so that a more detailed risk assessment can be made. On the generic proforma, health and safety issues can be identified underneath a list of any particular resources needed for the unit.

DIFFERENTIATED EXPECTATIONS

In this section, you would briefly indicate the level of attainment (expressed as a National Curriculum level or examination grade) you expect of the different ability groups within your class. In this way, you are setting targets for groups of students based upon your knowledge of the class. The (three) notional ability groups are broken down in the following terms:

1. 'After completing the unit, **most** students will have': this is what you expect of the majority of the class; the core, the key concepts and basic skills related to an appropriate level of attainment.

2. 'After completing the unit, **some students will not have made as much progress** and will': this is where you indicate the level at which you expect the less able in the class to achieve; this may arise out of a different task for these students.

3. 'After completing the unit, **some students will have progressed further** and will': this is where you indicate what you expect the most able to achieve; this may arise out of a different task or extension work with additional content.

This model of setting differentiated expectations in medium-term plans was developed by the Qualifications and Curriculum Authority (QCA) in their exemplar units of work for Key Stage 3. To look at examples in National Curriculum subjects go to **www.standards.dfes.gov.uk/schemes3/**

TEACHING APPROACHES

This column on the unit of work proforma provides some information about teaching strategies that have proved or will prove to be effective. For example, in relation to a particular activity or task, it may be that teacher modelling of a particular skill will be most effective; or perhaps the use of ICT would effectively consolidate children's understanding. The teaching strategies necessary to include all members of the teaching group should also be mentioned here.

Practical task

Use this medium-term planning proforma in the development of a unit of work you are going to teach. What are the strengths and weaknesses of this format and of using proformas in general?

Short-term planning: lessons

You will probably begin to develop lesson plans fairly early in your training. Two definitions are useful here:

- a lesson is a 'period for teaching something; an experience from which to learn';
- a plan is an 'arrangement for carrying out future activity; an arrangement of parts in a system'.

We have already made the obvious point that you – the teacher – are going to teach something that the students will learn. In this context, 'experience' refers to the methods or strategies that you use to connect what you want the students to learn to your assessment of that learning. The word 'arrangement' draws attention to the need to think carefully about the parts of a lesson; in what order do you put the experiences? How does the order influence the students' learning? In turn, that starts to take you back to the medium-term plan (unit of work) because a lesson plan comes from within this overview plan. A lesson plan is part of a sequence.

Although each lesson plan must be related to what has gone before and show how it is related to what is to come, it can appear to stand by itself. But it is a plan, not a script: it is something you work *from* and not *to*. There is the danger of planning too much and too little: too much detail can lead to you telling rather than teaching; too little can lead to a lack of focus in the teaching and to under-developing what it is you want the students to learn.

An effective short-term (lesson) plan should:

- **identify in detail what students should learn (the objectives);**
- **identify how you will know that progress has been made (the outcomes);**
- **identify opportunities and strategies for assessing the learning outcomes;**
- **show how lessons will start, end and continue;**
- **outline activities which show what students will do, how they will be grouped and what resources will be used;**

- identify key teaching points and key questions;
- show how students' learning can be supported or extended (differentiation);
- note how any support staff will be deployed.

Once again, this probably sounds like a daunting and unrealistically detailed list. In the example of lesson planning that comes at the end of this chapter, you will see how these requirements can be met manageably and meaningfully. At the moment, please remember that a lesson plan isn't a script nor is it an essay. It must be useful to you and allow an outside observer or examiner to understand what − and how − you have been teaching.

Practical task

Referring to the checklist above, use ICT to prepare a lesson plan format that you would find useful in your specialist subject.

DIFFERENTIATION

For a more detailed discussion of differentiation and inclusion, see Chapter 10.

This aspect of planning involves matching your tasks or activities and your teaching approaches to the needs and interests of the children in your classroom. At this point, however, it will be useful to note some principles of differentiation as they would impact upon a lesson plan.

In planning lessons as in planning units, it is useful to think about a core of learning that you will plan for all students in a class. This would consist of the key concepts and basic skills. Based upon your assessment of all students' likely progress against this 'core', you may also plan for two eventualities.

1. A 'support loop' that could involve a different task or activity, a different teaching approach or the support of another adult for those who may have difficulties; it is essential that any other adults are aware of your plans before the lesson and what you see as their role in supporting an individual or small group.

2. Extension activities for those who will be able to progress further, which may involve additional content of greater challenge, more independent research or the development of higher order skills such as synthesis, evaluation or application to different situations.

On lesson plans, these strategies can be related to individual students by name. If a student has been assessed at Stage 2 or above of the Code of Practice for Special Educational Needs, you will need to refer to their Individual Education Plan (IEP) when planning differentiated work (see Chapter 10 for more information on planning for students with special educational needs).

ASSESSMENT

You will need to give some details of the assessment opportunities (what and who?) and the assessment strategies (how?) employed during the lesson. Assessment strategies could take the form of monitoring a few individuals and discussing their contributions to a whole-class discussion, observing a specific student at work, a question and answer session with a small group, reading any written work produced during the lesson or marking homework or classwork after the class. You will also need to be aware of the record-keeping requirements of your department and how your ongoing assessment of students' progress will need to be recorded. The next chapter in this book deals with assessment of — and *for* — learning in some detail but for the moment, the key questions to address in lesson planning are:

For further information on assessment, see Chapter 4.

- **who** will your assessment activities focus on?
- **what** aspect of their work will you be assessing?
- **how** do you intend to achieve this?

MANAGING THE LESSON

An important aspect of planning a lesson involves thinking about the various stages or elements in the lesson's structure and the transitions between them. This will include the organisation of students (how they are grouped) and resources. The most common structure to lessons in secondary schools (especially at Key Stage 3) has three parts.

In the **introduction**, the teacher:

- **provides a clear, brisk start to the lesson;**
- **makes the purpose of the lesson and your expectations clear (very often, especially at Key Stage 3, this will involve sharing the objectives with the class explicitly);**
- **recaps on previous work;**
- **has strategies for ensuring all students take part;**
- **introduces key ideas through exposition, modelling, example, etc.;**
- **makes a smooth transition to the main part of the lesson.**

During the **development/main activity**, the teacher:

- **ensures students know what they are to learn;**
- **gives students a deadline for completion of work;**
- **ensures students know where to obtain resources, get help or receive further work;**
- **maintains pace by motivating students and keeping them on task;**
- **concludes main activity smoothly and moves to conclusion/plenary.**

In the **conclusion** or plenary, the teacher:

- **summarises important facts or key ideas;**
- **identifies what needs to be remembered for the next lesson;**
- **sets homework (if appropriate).**

A **plenary** may also involve the teacher managing:

- **students presenting and explaining their work;**
- **students generalising a rule from a number of examples;**
- **students reflecting on and evaluating how they have been working.**

For further
guidance on
managing
behaviour for
learning, see
Chapter 5.

MANAGING BEHAVIOUR FOR LEARNING

The justifiable assumption of this book is that if the teacher matches tasks or activities and teaching approaches to the needs and preferred learning styles of the students, then the potential for off-task or disruptive behaviour can be minimised. This applies to both 'ends' of the ability scale and the bored and unchallenged able children pose just as great a disruptive threat as the confused and frustrated less able.

Evaluation

Evaluations of learners' progress and your own effectiveness as a teacher will form the basis of written evaluations of your lessons. 'Good' lesson evaluations are honest and constructive and draw upon the student assessment information you have gathered during the lesson. The two most important evaluative questions that should be answered at the end of every lesson are:

1. To what extent were the learning objectives achieved?

2. Based on your assessment, what needs to be planned/taught next and why?

For further
information on
the link
between
assessment
and planning,
see Chapter 4.

Your answers to these questions will have a direct influence on your planning for the next lesson and, indeed, for the remaining lessons in the series.

Sometimes, trainees are asked to complete a more detailed evaluation of their teaching on a weekly basis that will be used in meetings with their mentor or tutor to set targets. An example of such an extended evaluation form from one training provider is reproduced in Figure 3.

Practical task

Complete the evaluation proforma in Figure 3 yourself at the end of a week's teaching. Use your evaluation as the basis of a meeting with your mentor. What aspects of teaching and learning will you focus on next week (e.g. structure, timing and pace, or assessment opportunities)?

A practical example

The following account of the lesson planning process was given by a PGCE (secondary) geography trainee near the end of her first (short) block school experience at an 11–16 technology college.

Context

'This was the first of seven lessons with a bottom set Year 10, looking at tourism as an economic system. We would be studying the UK (as an example of a more economically developed country [MEDC]) and Kenya (a less economically developed country [LEDC]).

Secondary QTS Weekly Evaluation

Trainee's name:	Classes taught:

1. Planning and preparation

Did my lesson planning adequately cater for the activities and content of the lessons? How effective was my preparation?

2. Planned learning objectives and outcomes

How realistic were they? To what extent were they achieved?

3. Teaching and learning methods

How effective were my teaching methods in bringing about student learning?

4. Structure, timing and pacing

How effective were these?

5. Management and resources

How effective was my classroom management and the use of resources?

6. Students' tasks

Did I introduce points clearly? To what extent did students understand them? Did I provide opportunities for students to contribute to discussion.

7. Behaviour management

How effective was it? To what extent was I able to motivate the students?

8. Use of Information and Communication Technology

Did I exploit the availlable oportunities to enhance students' learning through the appropriate use of ICT? Did I exploit the potential of ICT to help me in planning, preparation, recording and presenting information?

9. Assessment opportunities

Did I share the criteria for assessment with the students? How did I provide feedback to students on the quality of work? Did I encourage student self-evaluation?

10. Individual students/students

Comment as appropriate on the progress of individual students

11. Future planning

What implications does this evaluation have for my future planning? What will be my focus for the next set of lessons?

Figure 3: Evaluation proforma.

Exploring economic systems — different types (i.e. farming, industry and tourism) at different scales (national, international, global) — was one of the themes of the GCSE syllabus (OCR C) used by this school.

The class had completed farming and begun industry when I came to teach them. Their class teacher suggested I finish the section on industry by looking at Japan as a case study of an MEDC industrialised nation. From there I could take the class through tourism to complete the economic systems unit.

I taught two of the set's three lessons a week and could plan the lessons singularly or as a unit, spreading tasks across the two lessons. I would use the latter part of the second lesson to lead in to whatever the regular class teacher would be teaching.'

The planning process — first stage

'• Establish how many lessons available/required to teach the particular unit/topic.
• Establish students' prior knowledge and level of attainment.
• Establish the Key Questions that would need to be answered in this, the first lesson.
• Set out the Learning Objectives for the lesson based on answering the Key Questions. The Learning Objectives are divided into three categories:

1. Knowledge and Understanding.
2. Skills.
3. Values.

• Establish what Learning Outcomes are expected for All, Most and Some of the pupils.
• Identify assessment opportunities where I can establish whether learning outcomes have been achieved.

The importance of establishing students' prior learning and assessing learning outcomes were drummed into us at an early stage in the PGCE course, so these issues are uppermost in my mind during the planning process. Coming to a class for the first time, I obviously talk with the regular class teacher to establish what they have been covering. Once in the classroom, the start of each lesson acts as a review of the previous lesson (usually through a question and answer session, sometimes teacher talk) as well as an introduction to what is coming. I also use Q&As as a method of informal (formative) assessment of learning outcomes during and at the end of lessons. When students are working on tasks, I am able to carry out formative assessment through talking with individuals or groups to establish their level of understanding.

Having established the lesson content (**what** I want to teach) — which I find to be a quick and easy process — my main effort goes into planning **how** to teach it. This is the most time-consuming, challenging and creative element of planning.'

The planning process – second stage

'• Establish method or methods of teaching the content – in this case I decided on a multi-task worksheet as the main focus of the lesson.
• Work out how this worksheet would be taught – I considered the questions and explanations I would use.
• Establish rough timings for the lesson outline.
• Establish an introduction that would link previous learning to this new topic and provide transition into worksheet tasks.
• Assessment and SEN 'built-in' to the planning process – these were integral to my planning, e.g. I was conscious of having to meet needs of the least able students when considering the language of the worksheet.
• Literacy/Numeracy opportunities – Language use (mine and students'; written and verbal) always uppermost in my mind when planning. Numeracy opportunities were something of a bonus at this early stage in my teaching practice.
• Key Skill/Sustainable Development issues were 'add ons' – e.g. I would look at what I had planned and see if it addressed any sustainable development issues.
• Spiritual, moral, social, cultural (SMSC) development– this was another area I was aware I needed to address but, once again, I looked at it after most or all of the planning was done, rather than building it into the lesson.

The phrase 'joined-up' planning sprang to mind as I progressed through my first teaching practice. The more I planned, the more aware I became of how to include all the elements required – assessment, literacy, numeracy etc. At the beginning, all my energies went in to ensuring I knew what I wanted to teach and how to teach it. But pretty quickly, it became clear how all the apparently disparate elements fitted into a lesson, and into lesson planning. Now as I approach my second block of teaching practice, I feel even more confident about building in such elements as sustainable development and even SMSC development.'

Commentary on the lesson planning

This is a detailed lesson plan that uses a format developed to meet the needs of a secondary geography trainee. The evaluation at the end of the plan begins to address the two key, evaluative questions discussed earlier. The trainee's mentor or tutor would want to gather the following additional information when making any judgement about achieving the QTS Standards.

• **When will the trainee take the assessment opportunities mentioned (at what point in the lesson) and who (which students) will be her focus?**
• **The lesson indicates a rapid succession of activities during the lesson. Is sufficient time being allowed to develop students' understanding?**
• **The evaluation indicates that the students did not complete the worksheet and that this was anticipated. How can the trainee ensure that the final part of the lesson (termed 'recap') was effective in consolidating and extending all students' learning if they have either not completed the task or have reached a different stage?**

Topic Tourism (1)	**Set** GCSE Year 10
Date 5/12/03	

KEY QUESTIONS
Introduction to tourism as an economic system.
What is tourism – background, impact of recent events on tourist industry? Recent trends.
How does time/distance influence tourist activities?

LEARNING OBJECTIVES	**LEARNING OUTCOMES**
Kn/U: • Know that tourism is an economic system – that tourism is big business at various scales (UK and global). • Know and understand the recent trends in tourism – that more UK people travel abroad than holiday at home. • Know what factors have contributed to growth in tourism. • Understand time/distance impact on tourist activities & destinations. *Skills:* • Text and graph analysis *Values:* • Appreciate how big a contributor tourism is to the UK economy (jobs, money etc) & impact of recent events on tourist industry.	• All will know that tourism is big business and importance to the economy. • All will know and some will understand the various factors influence growth in tourism. • All/most will understand that greater distances can now be travelled in short space of time, opening up more areas to more people. • Most will appreciate that tourism affected by economy (recession/boom) and other events (Sept.11).

Teaching/learning strategies
Teacher talk, Q&A, individual work on worksheet tasks.

Resources/materials
Worksheets, whiteboard, textbook, OHP.

Language for learning/numeracy opportunities
Writing frame for those who need help with writing organisation; encouragement to use bullet points/spider diagrams ('brainstorms').

Citizenship/sustainable development
Tourism as a model of sustainable development.

Differentiation
By outcome, teacher intervention.

Assessment opportunities
Informal/formative – through Q&A, written work in class.

Homework	**Evaluation**
None set.	Good. Lesson objectives largely met. The last one was not addressed, as we did not reach that stage on the worksheet – however, I had not expected to finish all the questions. These will be continued in next lesson. Used whiteboard for written reinforcement of verbal instructions (page numbers etc). Tried to make explanations as clear as possible. Most of the class worked well, got on with tasks.

Time	**Lesson Outline**
2-3 mins	Register/settle
3-4 mins	Intro lesson objectives – tourism as an economic system; a tertiary (service) industry. Quick talk/Q&A about recent events affecting tourist trade (terrorism, foot and mouth).
2 mins	Intro tasks, hand out task sheets and textbooks. Do tasks one at a time.
5 mins	Task 1 – Importance of tourism to LEDC and MEDC. Discussion and whiteboard.
5+ mins	Task 2 – Holiday trends at home and abroad. Q&A, explanation.
10 mins	Task 3 – Leisure time OHT. Hand out writing frame. Go through factors on OHT and direct pupils to textbook. Pupils to write out factors in frame or as bullet points, spider diagram, sentences.
10 mins	Task 4 – Other factors. Go through OHT. Recap on this lesson's learning objectives and flag up next lesson's tasks.
1 min before bell.	Pack up and orderly departure.

This information would be gathered through lesson observation, discussions with the trainee and students and an examination of the worksheet designed by the trainee. Overall, it is clear that this trainee is beginning to consider the myriad aspects of planning for learning and beginning to integrate these in her lesson plans without undue anxiety or the production of over-detailed scripts.

Practical task

Work with your mentor as she or he plans a lesson in the format you devised earlier for your own lesson planning. Ask your mentor questions about the decisions they are making. This will help them to complete an activity that they will find fairly difficult (having already internalised a planning structure) and will help you to understand the planning process.

Then, observe the lesson being taught and notice how your mentor adapts the plan during the lesson. Make notes about the adaptations and changes and speculate on the reasons for them. After the lesson, discuss your notes with your mentor.

Planning for learning: a summary of key points

- *Effective planning builds on high expectations of students informed by a knowledge of their past and current achievements.*

- *Effective planning clearly identifies what is to be learned and the teaching strategies by which this will be achieved.*

- *Effective planning identifies the means by which learning will be assessed.*

- *Trainees need a good knowledge of their specialist subject so that they can plan over the long, medium and short term, ensuring student progression.*

- *Trainees need to be able to demonstrate the ability to plan for the development of students' learning across the curriculum, promote active and independent learning, and intellectually engage their students.*

Further reading

Ofsted (2002) *Good Teaching, Effective Departments*. This report presents the findings from a HMI survey of subject teaching in secondary schools during 2000–2001. There are many practical implications for trainees and mentors arising out of this report, including comments on planning for learning and managing teaching time.

Kyriacou, C. (1998) *Essential Teaching Skills* (2nd ed.). Cheltenham. Stanley Thornes. The second edition of this popular book covers a wide range of topics, including planning and managing lessons; classroom climate and discipline; streaming and setting; assessment, and continuing professional development.

For further information on planning for learning, visit **www.learningmatters. co.uk/education/learnteach/chapt3.html**

4 ASSESSMENT FOR LEARNING

JANE BRIGGS AND VIV ELLIS

Professional Standards for QTS

→ 2.1, 3.1, 3.1.3, 3.1.8, 3.2.6, 3.3.1, 3.3.2, 3.3.3, 3.3.4, 3.3.5, 3.3.6, 3.3.7, 3.3.8

To be awarded QTS you need to be able to use a range of strategies to assess students' learning. You will use your assessment knowledge to plan appropriately for the range of learning needs in your classes. You will be able to identify how you assess, both during the course of teaching and after teaching. Your subject knowledge will be crucial, as it will enable you to analyse the students' learning and make decisions about what is to be taught next, and how it should be taught. You will focus sharply on how you take the students' learning forward. You will be aware of the importance of the quality of interaction between you and your students and of the need for explicit oral and written feedback. Your record keeping should help you reflect on students' progress and attainment and should also enable you to report to parents, carers and other parties involved in the students' education. You will need to use your knowledge and understanding of comparative data to help you make informed decisions about how such data relates to your own teaching. In order to teach effectively, you will recognise how central assessment is to teaching and learning.

You may find it helpful to read through the appropriate section of the handbook that accompanies the standards for the Award of QTS for clarification and support.

What do we mean by assessment?

Assessment is the process by which teachers analyse students' learning. It is central to the activity of teaching. In 1988, a group of experts given the task of devising an assessment framework for what was to become the first National Curriculum, put it this way:

> The assessment process itself should not determine what is to be taught and learned. It should be the servant, not the master, of the curriculum. Yet it should not simply be a bolt-on addition at the end. Rather, it should be an integral part of the education process, continually providing both 'feedback' and 'feedforward'. It therefore needs to be incorporated systematically into teaching strategies and practices at all levels. Since the results of assessment can serve a number of different purposes, these purposes have to be kept in mind when the arrangements for assessment are designed.
>
> (TGAT 1988, p. 4)

You will see this quotation in a good deal of writing about assessment. To an extent, it has become a definitive statement. Often, however, its meaning and its importance are not immediately grasped by trainee teachers. Assessment has come to mean all sorts of things. Perhaps, most commonly, the term is used to describe the practices of awarding marks or grades to students' work and recording these. Assessment in its full sense, however, is so much more. The purpose of this chapter is to familiarise you with the various aspects of educational assessment and to demonstrate the relationship between assessment and the processes of teaching and learning.

The various aspects of assessment

What follows is a brief overview of the various aspects of assessment that have come to be included in this umbrella term. There are suggestions for further reading about key aspects of assessment at the end of this chapter.

TEACHER ASSESSMENT

In its general sense, this is the ongoing analysis of students' learning that is the day-to-day life-blood of good teaching. By observing, reading, questioning and interpreting students' comments and actions, teachers learn whether students are learning what they had intended them to learn. This process is constantly influencing an effective teacher's interventions in the classroom with students and this is how a teacher's lesson plans are adapted as those lessons are being taught.

Teacher assessment is a term that is also used to refer to the judgements teachers make about students' attainment in National Curriculum levels at the end of Key Stage 3 and is contrasted with and reported separately from the levels students are awarded through the externally marked national tests.

STUDENT SELF-ASSESSMENT

This term refers to students' involvement in the assessment process. It begins with students understanding the learning intentions or objectives for the particular lesson and the success criteria for the specific task or activity. It develops into students' awareness of their own strengths and weaknesses in a particular subject (and as a learner in general) and the ability to identify their own 'next steps' or targets. It may include a formal review of the students' work over a period of time – perhaps using a target-setting or progress review document – at which teacher and student identify progress, negotiate future targets and then report these to parents or carers.

FORMAL TESTS

There is no shortage of formal tests or examinations in the secondary phase. Some – like the optional national tests for Year 7 designed by QCA – are fairly new. Others – like GCSE – have been around for a comparatively long time. Here is a list of some of the formal tests you may encounter in schools:

- **standardised tests such as CATS (Cognitive Abilities Tests) or tests of reading and spelling ability;**
- **school (internal) examinations such as end-of-unit tests or annual end-of-year examinations;**
- **optional 'Progress' tests for Year 7 in Literacy and Numeracy that are designed and published by QCA but marked by schools;**

- **End of Key Stage 3 National Tests (often referred to as 'SATS') in the core National Curriculum Subjects of English, maths and science that are marked externally;**
- **GCSE and other 'intermediate' national examinations taken at the end of Key Stage 4 that lead to certification;**
- **the multiplicity of post-16 examinations.**

 Further information on the examination system from 14-19, see Chapter 9.

RECORD-KEEPING

Teachers are required to keep records of students' progress and attainment in school subjects. At the very least, this will probably take the form of recording whether a significant activity or task has been undertaken and the level of attainment. Some schools may issue teachers with customised documents or portable electronic devices in which to keep assessment records and marks; teachers in other schools may rely on their own mark books or 'teacher's planner'. You will need to find out about the expectations and requirements of your school. Assessment records should also provide teachers with information that can be used in their own forward-planning or in planning that takes place in departments across year groups.

TARGET-SETTING

There are several different layers to target-setting, all of which are designed to make the action required to raise standards explicit, to designate who is responsible for the action and the date by which progress will be reviewed.

- **LEA targets are determined by local education officers as a means of monitoring and raising standards of achievement across groups of schools and may be expressed as the number of students expected to achieve a particular level in an end of key stage test by a particular date.**
- **School targets are negotiated between LEA and the school's management team and, once again, may be expressed in terms of the percentage of a year group achieving five or more GCSEs at grade C or above.**
- **Curriculum targets are negotiated between a school's management team and a head of department or curriculum manager and would take into account past performance, student ability and the school's own targets.**
- **Student targets are negotiated between teacher and child following a review of the child's work; the student should be able to monitor their own progress and identify areas for future development; this is an aspect of student self-assessment mentioned earlier.**

REPORTING

You can probably remember your own school reports and may be surprised at how much they have changed over the last few years. Annual reports to parents and carers (including, for example, the End of Key Stage 3 test and Teacher Assessment results) now also detail strengths and areas for improvement in addition to the standards achieved.

USE OF COMPARATIVE DATA

Data means information and includes national and local End of Key Stage test results (KS2 and KS3) and GCSE results so that comparisons can be made between LEAs and between schools. Within school, the data can be used to identify trends with a view to setting curriculum and teaching targets; this will be increasingly important as you develop your career in schools.

At the moment, however, your first priority as a trainee is to develop the ability to analyse students' learning and to use the information you gather to inform your planning and teaching. By regarding assessment as an integral part of teaching you will be able to provide the continuous 'feedback' and 'feedforward' that are essential for effective student learning.

Why and how do teachers assess?

To take learning forward

> There is a firm body of evidence that formative assessment is an essential feature of classroom work and that development of it can raise standards.
>
> (Black and Wiliam 1998, p. 19)

As an integral part of the process of teaching and learning, assessment that is used to take students' learning forward can be described as 'formative assessment'. Teachers assess students' learning on a daily basis in order to be able to respond appropriately to their learning needs. Formative assessment is concerned with analysing students' comments and their answers to questions. It is concerned with listening to what students have to say and the way in which they go about a task. It is concerned with really looking at tangible end-products to find out what students know, understand and can do. It involves responding to information gained about students' learning during the course of teaching and afterwards to inform future teaching. Formative assessment means analysing, reflecting and acting in ways which will take students' learning forward. Formative assessment is an integral part of the interaction between teacher and students, informs future planning and teaching and provides information which enables the quality of teaching and learning to be evaluated.

We can therefore, consider formative assessment as being:

- **the analysis of students' learning and appropriate response during the course of teaching;**
- **the analysis of students' learning and appropriate response after the teaching episode.**

THE ANALYSIS OF STUDENTS' LEARNING AND APPROPRIATE RESPONSE DURING THE COURSE OF TEACHING

During teaching, you will be assessing students' learning continuously. Shipman (1983) describes this as:

> the thinking-on-the-feet that is one of the main skills of teaching.
>
> (Shipman 1983, p. 12)

While teaching, you will be interpreting what the students say and do in order to make judgements about their achievements. The ability to analyse the students' learning is vital if you are to make appropriate teaching points which help the students develop their knowledge and/or competence. You will be using your subject knowledge to help you identify what to look for and where to take the student next. You will need to listen, observe and question in ways which will enable you to give appropriate feedback or further instruction. It is crucial that feedback to students is explicit and indicates to them what they have achieved and how they can progress further. It is also crucial that you are able to interact with students in ways which enable them to take risks: you will discover much from students' errors and misconceptions. The ability to respond immediately, providing appropriate feedback and further teaching, can be much more meaningful for that child than waiting to the next day when the moment has passed. This is sometimes referred to as monitoring and the Professional Standards for the Award of QTS refer to 'Monitoring and Assessment'.

Black and Wiliam (1998) highlight the importance of assessment being used to enhance teaching and therefore to raise standards. They argue that the real way to raise standards is to improve the quality of teaching by enhancing teachers' ability to use formative assessment in the classroom. The Assessment Reform Group explores these issues further in *Assessment for Learning:Beyond the Black Box* (1999), including discussions about the involvement of students within the assessment process and the impact this can have on their motivation and self-esteem. They also stress the importance of teachers asking the right questions in order to analyse effectively.

Classroom story

In a Year 7 maths lesson, the teacher was revising area and perimeter. The students were asked to find the measurement in centimetres of one side of a rectangle. They were shown a diagram of the rectangle on which the area had been written in (10cm squared) and the height (2cm). The students were asked to write their answers on their individual whiteboards and hold them up for the teacher to see. One child had written '3cm'. The teacher asked: 'Explain to me how you got that answer. How did you work it out?' The child explained: 'I added 2cm and 2cm to get 4cm. Then I took 4cm away from 10cm which left 6cm. Then I divided 6cm by 2 which gave me 3.' From this the teacher clearly realised that the child was confusing perimeter and area.

She then explained to the child what she thought he had done – that he had thought the perimeter was 10cm and used that information to work out the length of the rectangle. She repeatedly asked questions such as : 'Is that what you were thinking?' and 'Is that right?'. She then explained that 10cm squared was the area, drawing the cm squares onto the diagram to illustrate her teaching point. She demonstrated how to work out the length of the rectangle by counting the cm squares. Next, she asked the child: 'Can you explain to me the difference between perimeter and area?' He was able to explain that one was 'the total distance around the outside edge of the shape' and the other was 'the surface of the shape', pointing at the diagram appropriately as he spoke.

The teacher then demonstrated how to work out the area of the shape by multiplying the length by the height, writing on the board : '5cm x 2cm = 10cm'. She then reminded the student of the inverse operation : 10 divided by 2 = 5 and explained how to use the information about the area of an rectangle to find out details of the length of the sides. She carried out two more similar examples with the whole class, checking that everyone, and particularly that one boy, had the correct answer.

This example demonstrates how teachers need to ask the right questions in order to analyse students' misconceptions and errors. By using the whiteboard the teacher could see the child's error and respond immediately to rectify the misunderstanding rather than the child completing several examples incorrectly during the lesson and not learning of the mistake until the work had been marked and returned at a later stage. The teacher was able to make appropriate teaching points based on her analysis of the student's response to the task. In this, her questioning was vital.

THE ANALYSIS OF STUDENTS' LEARNING AND APPROPRIATE RESPONSE AFTER THE TEACHING EPISODE

In order to evaluate your teaching and to make decisions about what to teach next and how, you will need to reflect upon the students' learning and make judgements about their attainment. Analysis after teaching will include looking at samples of the students' work, reflecting on their comments and actions and may also involve discussions with colleagues. It may be that you need to amend your plans to clarify misconceptions or to raise the level of challenge. It may be that you need to develop your own subject knowledge further in order to enhance the quality of experience offered to the students. You will need to think about the feedback which you will give to the students and how this can motivate them to further their own achievements. Assessment knowledge will, therefore, be used to inform future teaching and if used effectively should *enhance* future learning.

Formative assessment, then, can be defined as the process by which teachers make judgements about students' attainment and use this information to inform teaching and learning and planning in order to take students' learning forward. Involving students is a key element of formative assessment. Explicit feedback enables students to recognise what is required of them and how they can progress. They need to have ownership of their own learning and need to be able to identify their successes and areas for development. Students need to engage in meaningful dialogue with their teachers to reflect upon their learning and to work together effectively.

Classroom story

During a Year 7 unit of work on poetry, an English trainee had been working on the production of individual poetry anthologies with the class. He used the marking of these anthologies to inform his teaching in the remainder of the unit and to give positive and constructive feedback to the students that could inform the extended piece of writing they would prepare towards the end of the unit. His marking appears below:

Jane, your work was perfectly presented. I like the way you chose appropriate colours for each poem, eg, seaweed green near the lines about the stomach!

In your comments on the poems, your ideas are first-rate. I particularly liked your comparison of the sea to a 'plaything' for a child and where you examined how this brought to mind ideas of 'harmlessness' — why not think a little more about this idea by considering the question mark that comes after it? What effect does the poet achieve by placing the question mark here?

Although I thought you'd completed the difficult part of this task well, I don't think you were as successful with the easier part. When you are expressing your opinions about poetry, a good way of justifying these to a reader is by using quotations from the poem (as we discussed). So, although you say the writer compares the sea to beautiful things, you don't say that the phrase 'it runs in beads on their jackets' made you think this. We will work on this in readiness for the final piece of writing in the unit.

The trainee's marking is specific and focused on the student's work. It identifies positive achievements and demonstrates to the student that he has read and engaged with her work. The trainee has also identified an important skill that the student will need to develop and how this relates to what he plans to teach next.

In his marking of the completed individual poetry anthology, the trainee is beginning to engage in a dialogue with his students. This dialogue was developed during part of a lesson when the trainee worked with groups of students to review their marked work while the remainder of the class worked on an independent activity. Over a period of three lessons, the trainee had seen all the students about their work and used the marking as the basis for a dialogue about improvement.

Practical task

From a lesson or lessons you have taught, identify examples of:

a. your analysis of students' learning and your appropriate response during teaching; consider your use of questioning, explaining, demonstration, etc;

b. your analysis of students' learning and appropriate response after teaching; consider how assessment influenced your future teaching and was reflected in your plans.

In both cases, how did your assessment enhance your teaching and what impact did it have on the students' learning?

To make judgements about standards

Summative assessment is more commonly associated with testing or making judgements about students' overall achievement at the end of a period of time. It requires students to demonstrate their knowledge, skill or understanding as a means of what Harlen, Gipps, Broadfoot and Nuttall (1994) describe as 'summing up and checking up'. They describe the former as:

> a picture of current achievements derived from information gathered over a period of time in order to set future targets.
>
> (Harlen, Gipps, Broadfoot and Nuttall 1994, p. 223)

This picture of student achievement can be used to inform students of progress and to set future targets. It can also be used by teachers to reflect upon the quality of teaching and to inform future planning. Since the introduction of the National Curriculum and its assessment, teachers have increasingly been required to make judgements about standards of attainment within a criterion – referenced system. Barrs (1990) highlights the impact this can have when teachers' assessment practice becomes that of measuring attainment of previously identified criteria rather than considered analysis of students' learning.

With the current emphasis on national test results forming a key part of political agendas, the judgement of standards is more commonly linked to the evaluation of teaching performance. National test results are used as an indicator of school effectiveness and teacher performance. LEA and school targets influence the expectation of student attainment.

Information about standards of attainment can be considered from two key perspectives:

- **measuring progress and attainment;**
- **evaluating the effectiveness of schools.**

MEASURING PROGRESS AND ATTAINMENT

Your judgements about students' attainment over a period of time will enable you to consider whether progress has been made and to identify future learning targets. You will need to look closely at students' work to identify what improvements there have been: this will require you to draw on your subject knowledge. You will also need to develop your ability to identify the National Curriculum levels at which the students are operating. Your record-keeping should enable you to consider what progress students have made and should help you identify ways forward for individuals. It is important that your record-keeping system is manageable and that you can use it to further your understanding of students' progress and attainment.

Practical task

Examine examples of teachers' record keeping in your department. Consider the following:

- *How 'learning-specific' are they? What do they tell you about the students' knowledge, skills and/or understanding?*
- *How would these records enable you to take the students' learning forward? What information do they contain that could inform future teaching and planning?*
- *How would these records support reporting to parents/carers (in writing and orally)?*

The use of comparative data can help you identify trends and patterns in student attainment but you will need to consider the data carefully as it can be limited. Teachers are now expected to be aware of students' attainment in national tests and to use comparative data across key stages to monitor progress. Clearly, only that which has been tested can be considered and teachers need to be aware of the limitations of testing and the reliability and validity of the data provided.

EVALUATING THE EFFECTIVENESS OF SCHOOLS

Teachers are accountable to their students, their parents and carers, the school, the LEA and the wider community. Scrutiny of the standards of student attainment and their performance in national tests and examinations are key features of Ofsted inspections. This leads into an evaluation of the effectiveness of the school. Making simplistic comparisons between the examination results of different schools serving very different communities and with very different resources does not allow us to make valid judgements about the effectiveness of the teaching in those schools. For example, comparing the GCSE results of a selective grammar school in an affluent suburb with the results of a comprehensive school in a city where many students enter late in KS3 without fluency in English will not tell us much about the work that goes on in classrooms. To try to quantify the 'difference' made by teachers in schools, the notion of 'value-added' was developed whereby the effectiveness of teaching in a school is judged partly by the progress made by its students from a base-line assessment on entry to the school. Increasingly, school examination result league tables – and Ofsted and LEA reviews – are building in elements of 'value-added' assessment.

So what do trainee teachers need?

The Standards for the Award of QTS are a set of outcome statements that you must demonstrate. It is important to note that the Standards for Monitoring and Assessment come within Section 3 of the Standards that relates to Teaching: assessment takes its place between Planning and Teaching. The Assessment Standards make repeated connections with the ability to understand how students learn and how to plan lessons. It is in this spirit, therefore, that we offer the following list of skills and attributes that you will develop as an effective, beginning teacher:

- the ability to interpret students' learning using a variety of strategies appropriate to your subject;
- a confident knowledge of your specialist subject in which you take delight and pleasure so that you can re-formulate lesson content, answer questions and represent ideas in a way that is appropriate to the needs of the learners in your classroom;
- the ability to make assessment a continuous and integral part of your teaching so that the information gathered has an immediate effect upon your interventions in students' learning as well as informing future planning;
- the ability to ask the 'right' questions that check understanding rather than simple recall and probe misconceptions;
- the ability to implement a record-keeping system that is manageable and meaningful to yourself, other members of your department and school and that is open to parents and carers;
- an awareness of the implications of formal, national tests for curriculum planning and your own professional development;
- an awareness of the use of comparative data in setting targets and understanding how your students' performance compares with those in other classes and other schools.

Assessment for learning:

a summary of key points

____ *Assessment is an integral part of teaching and learning.*

____ *It is a process by which we make judgements about students' learning.*

____ *Effective formative assessment (including student self-assessment) is a key part of raising standards of attainment.*

____ *Summative assessment is used to measure students' progress and attainment, but also school effectiveness.*

____ *Trainee teachers need to be able to use their analysis of students' learning in a dialogue with parents, carers and others involved in the education of students.*

Further reading

Black, P. and Wiliam, D. (1998) *Inside the Black Box: Raising Standards Through Classroom Assessment.* London. King's College. This short pamphlet offers a review of research into the ways in which formative assessment can have an impact on the quality of teaching and learning in classrooms. The authors put forward an argument for the improvement of formative assessment in order to raise standards.

Gipps, C. and Stobart, G. (1997) *Assessment: A Teacher's Guide to the Issues*. London. Hodder and Stoughton. This well-respected guide is available in most education libraries and is written in a lively and accessible way. It covers a wide range of assessment issues, including fairness and validity in assessments, baseline and value-added measures, and the National Curriculum.

For further information on assessment for learning, visit **www.learning matters. co.uk/education/learnteach/chapt4.html**

5 MANAGING BEHAVIOUR FOR LEARNING

ALAN J. CHILD

Professional Standards for QTS

 1.1, 1.2, 1.3, 2.7, 3.3.1, 3.3.9

To be awarded QTS you must have high expectations of your students in terms of their work and behaviour. You must model high standards of respect and demonstrate positive values related to learning. You should know a range of strategies for managing student behaviour for learning in a safe and secure environment. You should recognise that some students' behaviour is influenced by complex factors outside the school and seek to manage these so that other students' learning is not adversely affected. You should be able to establish clear frameworks and manage students' behaviour constructively.

You may find it helpful to read through the appropriate section of the handbook that accompanies the Standards for the Award of QTS for clarification and support.

Introduction

This chapter title is an important emphasis in its own right because it is a natural instinct for a trainee teacher to seek to manage students' behaviour and then to focus on their learning. The key message is that the appropriate use of the knowledge and skills discussed in Chapters 2, 3 and 4 will enable the teacher to create a classroom climate in which the students' right to learn is matched by the teacher's right to teach.

Hardly a day passes without some horror story appearing in the press about the unacceptable behaviour of students in secondary schools. These headlines do not, of course, capture the reality in the vast majority of schools where students engage in learning and a culture of mutual respect exists. David Bell, Her Majesty's Chief Inspector of Schools, said recently:

> The proportion of schools in which the behaviour of students is unsatisfactory overall was less in the schools inspected in 2002/3 than in the previous year. Behaviour is judged to be at least satisfactory overall in the vast majority of schools, and good or better in nearly three quarters. Effective action to promote good behaviour is becoming more widespread. This includes setting and maintaining high expectations for behaviour; the consistent application of rewards and sanctions, and the use of timely and well-managed interventions. (HMCI Report 2002/3: 113)

In surveys conducted by the Teacher Training Agency (TTA) amongst newly qualified teachers (NQTs) 50 per cent of respondents maintain that the training they received in behaviour management was inadequate to meet their needs in the first year of teaching. Some 45 per cent of teachers who decide to leave the profession cite student indiscipline and lack of respect for the teacher as major reasons for their decision to pursue an alternative career. So, quite clearly, if you have some early concerns about how you will manage students' behaviour for learning, you are certainly not alone in experiencing some genuine uncertainty and perhaps a little trepidation at the prospect of working with a lively group of Year 11 students on a Friday afternoon on a wet and windy November day!

All the analysis and research into effective teaching emphasises that unacceptable behaviour is likely to be minimised when the teacher:

- **aims to personalise the learning for each student and identifies the most appropriate learning style;**
- **supports and challenges students as well as planning activities and content which are interesting;**
- **monitors and recognises progress based on well developed assessment strategies.**

In addition to these pedagogical principles, effective teachers employ a range of techniques to encourage students who are disengaging from the learning to re-engage and be 'on task'; the very best classroom practitioners anticipate students' 'off task' behaviour and take pre-emptive action. If you have observed an experienced and effective teacher at work with a demanding class you might have had a mixed reaction: sheer admiration as you watched this paragon manage the learning of thirty Year 9 students with good humour, effortless transitions from activity to activity and real pace and momentum; some despair as you reflect that such multi-skilled, multi-tasked teaching is beyond you – an impossible dream.

Every teacher, at some point in their career, experiences challenging student behaviours. Often, factors are at play which relate to the student's home circumstances or with social groupings and influences outside the school environment. Although teachers so readily accept responsibility and endure intense reflection wondering how this awful moment could have been avoided, you will also no doubt meet some cynical staffroom commentary which alludes to the past ('things were better then'), falling standards ('we used to have a discipline policy here'), and the decline in family and society values ('what do you expect when programmes like *Footballers' Wives* are on TV?'). You might also be tempted by the quick fix ostensibly offered by some of the burgeoning catalogue of classroom management textbooks. The idea of tips for teachers needs to be dispelled as, at best, they are a short term strategy. You can gain from reading around the subject of behaviour management but success in the classroom is not predicated simply on the deployment of techniques.

Praise

There is ample evidence to support the effectiveness of teacher praise in creating a positive classroom environment and in motivating students into behaviour for learning. This is not to say that the teacher who uses praise in a cosmetic, artificial way will be successful. Praise used in the appropriate way is indeed a powerful force; praise used insincerely will undermine relationships and learning.

There are three important aspects to consider:

Personal: praise should be given to the individual or group so that it resonates personally. The most obvious thing to do is to name the students and to ensure that they receive the praise in a direct way with, for example, positive non-verbal signals like a smile.

Specific: praise should be firmly grounded in a particular achievement or attainment which is clearly referred to. For example, if a student has finished a task which has previously caused difficulty, the teacher's compliment should specify that the praise is for finishing the task and for the effort to overcome the particular problem.

Genuine: praise must always be given to students who have really achieved something. The careless, repetitive use of praise will undermine the value of other praise you want to give. Imagine how you have felt when in the presence of someone who overuses the words 'thank you': in a short time they no longer ring true and can, indeed, become irritating!

Praise which is offered in close proximity to the achievement or attainment is usually the most well received and the most powerful in motivating students.

You might need to consider some less public ways to praise senior students. Year 10 and 11 students may not welcome the embarrassment of public acclaim in front of their classmates.

Practical task

Imagine that a student in your Year 10 group who has been an inconsistent performer achieves really well in a particular lesson, making useful contributions during small group discussion with four other students. You are delighted to witness this quality of work and engagement and you can see that the student has been motivated by the task. You also know that he has a reputation as 'one of the lads' and know that any public acknowledgement will not go down well and might even provoke disengagement in subsequent lessons.

Think of five ways you can privately praise an upper school student and still follow the three key principles of making the praise personal, specific and genuine (and in his case, private).

Rules and routines

It is increasingly common in a school to find that not only has it a behaviour management policy but also some clearly specified classroom rules prominently displayed on noticeboards. Additionally you may come across other documentation (probably in the staff handbook) which advises on anti-bullying, anti-racism, attendance, school uniform regulations and even a code of conduct or key principles. This material can be quite daunting and far from easy to absorb. It is important, however, to do some research and reading about the school's key policies and practice as you are working in a context and need to be in tune with its key concepts and the practicalities. For example, a school might have a sophisticated system to manage challenging student behaviours like an on-call scheme involving the support of senior staff; or it might have access to a facility like a retreat; or it might employ a school counsellor.

Practical task

In the school where you are working collect all the printed and published information relating to the management of student behaviour. Examine (trace) the links between the school's mission statement/school development plan and the rules and routines which operate on a daily basis: the school aspires to be a community which respects the environment and its members, but do staff and students work together to minimise litter? Do you see common courtesies exchanged between staff and students (a good place to observe is doorways and staircases)? Are the rules and routines followed and are they reinforced by staff? When you have gathered this data you might want to share your reflections with your school mentor or your college tutor. Do remember to respect the organisation in which you are training; it may feel defensive if you simply list the aspects in a purely negative way. A fruitful approach is to see if you can offer some ideas to improve the situation. A group of trainees can work as a 'think tank' and offer a joint analysis and action plan.

It can be a very reassuring and supportive environment if you undertake some of your training in a school which has very clearly expressed values, rules and routines. It can be very helpful if you work in a school where the staff have good relationships with students and can offer you insights into the effective management of learning for behaviour. You might, however, feel that the environment is so supportive that you are not actually developing your own skills but simply adopting the good practice of others. At the other end of the spectrum where you are left largely to your own devices, the challenge may be far too great and you may feel daunted and confused as you try to establish your classroom rules and routines.

Students do need the freedom to work within constraints. Classroom rules are an effective way to establish and develop the climate for learning. The general wisdom pertaining to classroom rules is that they should be:

- **developed and owned by the students and the teacher;**
- **few in number;**
- **expressed in positive language;**
- **about improving learning;**
- **reinforced and reviewed regularly.**

A classroom behaviour plan

You might find it useful to think about an overall approach for your classroom under several headings:

1. Movement.
2. Learning.

3. Communication.
4. Mutual respect.
5. Safety.
6. Problem-solving.

If you do this you will think about how students enter and leave your classroom, how they will work in groups, noise levels, common courtesies, using equipment and how to deal with challenges.

Practical task

Working with another trainee, develop five 'golden rules' for the classroom. Remember to phrase them positively and to produce rules which encourage behaviour for learning. Why not share these with other members of your group?

You might like to compare your proposals with those you have seen published in your placement schools.

Consequences

In most schools, unacceptable student behaviour incurs a consequence. Commonly, schools operate reward strategies and a hierarchical set of sanctions. As a trainee it can be rather disconcerting to find yourself working in a school without a full appreciation of the systems. If you act idiosyncratically, the students will undoubtedly react, or possibly overreact, to your sanctions. Therefore, it is essential to know and follow the school's protocols. This can be a source of some tension if you find yourself working within a system that does not attune with your own values and beliefs. As you become more skilled in managing behaviour for learning you might feel that the school's approach is undermining your teaching style, or you might feel that the system offers insufficient support, or that you are not given sufficient independence by your mentor. Any one of these reactions is understandable but the school is a community in which you are a privileged guest and you should seek to integrate as fully as possible with its modus operandi. However, your own professional development can certainly be enhanced by careful reflection on the contexts in which you are working and perhaps through discussion with other trainees and your college tutor. Good teachers give students choices and make clear to students the consequences of the choices they make. In an ideal world you would hope that the use of sanctions would be a small part of your work but there will be several occasions when you feel that a student is deserving of some consequence. The purpose of your intervention is to manage behaviour for learning so you need to think very carefully about the actions you take.

Practical task

In the table below there is a list of sanctions which are typically deployed in schools. For each one, identify the student behaviour that could invoke it and then consider the possible advantages and disadvantages of the teacher's action. Some commentary has been added to encourage your thinking.

Sanction	Student behaviour	Possible advantage/disadvantage
'See me at the end of the lesson.'		
Work to be repeated to a higher standard		
Verbal warning/ reprimand		
Written report to Head of Year		
Contact with parent/ carer		
Detention		Detentions at break, lunchtimes and after school are commonly used in schools. They are highly inconvenient to staff and often require considerable administration. What is the intended outcome?
Exclusion from the classroom		This should be a very rare event and in many schools is discouraged and only acceptable in extreme situations to avoid confrontation in front of the whole class.
Withdrawal of privileges		
Stern/disapproving look		Effective teachers are skilled at using non-verbal techniques. Sometimes the eyes can work wonders and get a student back on task without a word being spoken.
Moving student to another desk		
Issuing a bad conduct mark		

Teacher techniques

As a trainee teacher you are expected to know some of the techniques for managing behaviour for learning. You will learn these in a variety of ways: from your own reading, in workshops and by the careful observation of effective teachers. There are some techniques which have been identified by several researchers into effective teaching. They have been extensively written about, feature in many INSET sessions and form part of the ever-expanding literature on behaviour management. You may try some of these and find no or little success; others may work beautifully. The techniques themselves work best when other key aspects of pedagogy are present. But the classroom is above all else an environment where interpersonal relationships have pride of place. Students recognise when a teacher is knowledgeable, well prepared, the lesson has a clear learning focus and the teacher cares: they respond positively to a climate of learning. The techniques discussed in the next few paragraphs are certainly field-tested and effective but only if the foundations of good teaching are well established.

- **Tactical ignoring:** sometimes as a teacher you have to ignore some students' behaviour because if you respond then the flow of the lesson will be interrupted and your intervention will be more disruptive than the student's behaviour. This is never an easy judgement to make. Nor does it mean that you cannot speak to the offending student at a later stage.
- **Thank you:** acknowledging those who are on task can often encourage those who are still thinking about getting down to work to follow suit.
- **Redirecting:** rather than pointing out to students what they are not doing, you can simply reassert what 'we' are doing. 'Ismael and Alice, we are looking at the diagram on page 3, OK?'
- **Room to change:** it is often useful to draw a student's attention to what you would like them to do, then move away saying you'll check in a minute or two to see if they are on task. This gives the student a chance and room to do it without a stand-off or confrontation developing.
- **Location:** if you always teach from the front of the room you are wasting opportunities. Move around the room. Often, your proximity to a student or a group can encourage on-task behaviour and you don't need to say a word. (In taking different perspectives you also scan the room and may see things which were not visible in teaching from the front.)
- **Non-verbal signals:** effective teachers use a wide range of strategies which you may not be aware of as you observe them working with a group of students. You may be amazed at how a teacher uses eye contact to attract a student's attention or with a gentle smile indicates approval. Students are receptive to body language so you need to adopt a positive but not overbearing posture which exudes confidence. The appropriate use of a 'thumbs up' can send a strong message of approval as can a subtle nod; or the symbolic shaking of the head to indicate unacceptability. Sometimes to gain the attention of a whole class teachers can use signals to gain listening order: for example, standing at the front of the classroom with an outstretched arm pointing to the whiteboard can indicate your readiness to move to another activity. Some drama teachers count down from five to one (the five is loudly issued but not shouted and the following numbers are spoken with decreasing volume) and teach the class that at number one there is a listening silence.

Personal feelings

It is a cliché to observe that people have different reactions to different experiences. It can be quite challenging as a teacher when things do not go according to plan or when a student speaks to, or behaves towards, you in a manner which you find totally unacceptable. For some it could mean a really tearful moment; for others it could mean a groundswell of anger and frustration. And on a daily basis, of course, we have days when we feel a bit under the weather or the journey to work has been a stressful one with heavy traffic and delays. Teachers need to have a good sense of themselves and have to work hard at managing their emotional state so that it does not interfere with the business of teaching and learning. This is not to suggest that teachers are automata without feelings, delivering some sterile, bland curriculum in a highly prescriptive way, but you do need to look hard at yourself and use your 'emotional intelligence'.

Confrontation/challenging behaviours

These words evoke some of the horror images referred to in the introduction but you probably do want some advice on this area. One thing to bear in mind is the very language we use when we talk about student behaviour. It is important to agree definitions. For example, some writers talk about unacceptable behaviour, some use the phrase challenging behaviour and some refer to confrontational behaviour. There is, of course, a sliding scale from a student's refusal to follow a simple instruction to threatening the teacher's physical well-being (a very rare event indeed!)

As teachers we cannot control all the frustrations and pent-up emotions of our students, but we can try to equip them with the skills to express their anger effectively. If you encounter an angry student try these ideas:

- **Don't match the student's anger with your own. This leads to escalation. The student needs you to be calm as a palliative to their own anger.**

- **Be consistent in your response: express that you are not happy at being shouted out, respond to the behaviour and be specific.**

- **Offer the student a chance to talk about how they are feeling. You might suggest a cooling off period before they tell you more. Offer to be a listener; do not be judgemental.**

- **Point out the positives in their behaviour which you have seen previously: use this as a way to give genuine praise and work towards a resolution.**

- **Give space and room: do not invade the personal space of the challenging student.**

- **Speak calmly, clearly and ask questions which show a genuine wish to understand the problem.**

- **Deal with the behaviour and not the student.**

- **Remember that the challenge is probably not directed at you personally.**

- **Assistance should be available from other staff in the school. (Note: as a trainee you are under the supervision of a designated mentor who is legally responsible for your welfare. Technically, you are never responsible for the students in your classroom; that responsibility lies with the school that is hosting your training.)**

If this is an area where you feel you need further ideas, you will find some useful material in Paul Blum's *The Teacher's Guide to Anger Management* and in Michelle MacGrath's *The Art of Teaching Peacefully*.

It is important in these challenging moments to be able to control your own emotions so that they do not impede your ability to act professionally. This is easier said than done of course because the 'moment' is highly charged. Different actions trigger different responses in people as you well know, but you should begin to think through your own sensitivities so that you can manage them accordingly. Are you likely to overreact to a student who fails to extend the common courtesy of using 'Sir' or 'Miss'? Would a student ostentatiously chewing in your lesson invoke a major incident? Would you be very offended if you overheard a student using offensive language to their neighbour? How would you react if a student commented on your hairstyle or your clothing? Would you 'lecture' a student you found smoking because you are a non-smoker yourself? Would you be affronted if a student asked about your family or made a so-called witty comment about your ancient car?

Classroom story

A trainee teacher is having considerable difficulty with a Year 10 Set 1 English group who are studying Othello *for GCSE. The students are enjoying the play, and were particularly attentive whilst watching extracts from a film version starring Lawrence Fishburne. As soon as the trainee teacher tries to lead a whole class discussion, the students disregard the classroom conventions (and school policy) of orderly response. Students shout out answers and comments without waiting for permission. The trainee is unsure how to recover the situation without destroying the students' enthusiasm and obvious engagement with the text. There is nothing malicious in the students' behaviour but the trainee feels that there is a distinct lack of order: the students are manipulative but never rude.*

Understandably, the trainee decides that the next lesson will be more orderly and decides that the discussion about the film will continue but it will be done differently. In fact, the trainee decides that the classroom rule of students seeking permission to speak by raising their hands will be strictly followed. The trainee rightly plans to limit the discussion (it will only last for twenty minutes) and decides that the students will be told that a written task will follow the discussion.

Unfortunately, and rather predictably, the next lesson does not go as anticipated because the students simply refuse to accept the classroom rule about raising their hands and the trainee becomes increasingly wearied and irritated. The discussion becomes fragmented and disjointed because the trainee spends time and verbal energy trying to establish the 'new order'. Eventually, the trainee moves to the written task to restore acceptable levels of behaviour and tells students that they can expect more writing in future lessons unless their attitude and behaviour improves. The students do engage in the written task and the quality is good.

Practical task

Referring to the classroom story, try the miracle question technique. Imagine a fairy godmother is able to grant one wish to the trainee who is working with this Year 10 group! What would the trainee ask for?

To frame the question for the fairy godmother, the trainee needs to think carefully about the desired outcomes. There are some suggestions below.

Desired outcomes:

- *The students will answer questions and join in the discussion in an orderly way which gives everyone a chance to make a contribution.*

- *The students will listen carefully and politely to the contributions from others and learn from them.*
- *The students will respect the teacher's role in structuring the discussion and follow the established protocols.*
- *The discussion will enable the students to learn through reflection and debate.*
- *The students will be able to accept different views and opinions.*
- *The discussion will last long enough for key learning objectives to be achieved.*

The idea of the miracle question technique is to enable a problem to be changed into an achievable goal. Often, because of the intensity of the classroom with so many things happening simultaneously and a steady stream of interactions, the trainee may not be able to analyse the problem beyond the immediacy, for example, of irritation and disappointment with the non-co-operative students. The miracle question is a chance for fresh thinking and an opportunity to see a positive future. From this vision, it is possible to derive the possibilities and also to really see what the problem is.

So, what wish should this trainee put to the fairy godmother?!

Scaling

Another way to address classroom management issues which are causing you concern is to use a *scaling* technique. The trainee with the Year 10 English group might feel that chaos was the key feature of the lesson and that their authority has been undermined. Worse still they might have genuine dread at the thought of the next lesson: how can I restore my professional credibility? The truth is often hard to see when you are over-whelmed by emotions. It can be really helpful to analyse the situation, perhaps with the help of a mentor. Scaling is a simple strategy. Think of a scale of 1 to 10 with 1 repre-senting the lowest point and with 10 representing the highest point. You then attach a brief description to each point on the scale, decide where you are on that scale and consider steps to move you gradually up the scale: you are not trying to make a giant leap but small manageable steps towards a better situation. This is a really positive way to address concerns and helps you to see the wood for the trees!

Practical task

Refer again to the classroom story about teaching Othello.

There are three stages to this task:

(a) *Look at the scale which has been part completed. Can you attach description to points 7, 8 and 9?*
(b) *Now consider where on the scale you would place this Year 10 English class.*
(c) *Then, working with a mentor or another trainee, suggest one or two strategies which could be attempted to move the class one point up the scale in the conduct of whole class discussion.*

Point 10 is of course the ideal, but no teacher can move a class from point 1 to point 10 in some great miraculous leap!

1. *The students shout out, don't listen and much of the talk is irrelevant and designed to upset the teacher and prevent learning.*
2. *The teacher tries to follow the classroom rules but the students ignore them.*
3. *The teacher keeps having to stop the discussion to remind students about the rules for discussion; occasionally they are followed.*
4. *The students know the rules but break them because they want to be talking; the teacher has to be very firm on the rules and is unhappy that students are not learning and using them.*
5. *The students engage well with the topic and make lively contributions but it is rather chaotic, and certain students are dominating the discussion.*
6. *The teacher is taking a back seat for parts of the discussion because students are talking to/with each other in a fairly sensible way.*
... 7, 8, 9 – Describe these points on the scale.
10. *The class discuss the film in a mature way following all the conventions of debate and verbal exchange; the teacher is able to take a back seat and only occasionally intervene as a facilitator to move the discussion forward.*

This chapter has attempted to offer some guidance and support. There will be days when you feel that the your best plans for learning have fallen foul of things beyond your control, whether that be inclement weather or the distraction of a false fire alarm! Other days, your students will be responsive and engaged, you will see real progress and you will gain those rather intangible benefits ascribed to the 'buzz' of the successful classroom. As your competence and confidence grow you will become less conscious of managing behaviour for learning and the skilful blending of pedagogy and student and classroom management will be achieved almost without you knowing it. Good teachers, like good poets, borrow from each other: do not be afraid to try new ideas and new techniques acquired from other teachers or your own reading; do not be disappointed if what works one day is less effective on another. The successful teacher is innovative; the effective teacher is reflective and the very best make mistakes and learn from them.

Managing behaviour for learning:
a summary of key points

_____ *The management of behaviour is not a separate set of skills to be applied to students but an integral part of the teacher's role in enabling students to learn. That is why the chapter is entitled 'Managing behaviour for learning'.*

_____ *The climate of the classroom depends on key values and beliefs: paramount is that of mutual respect.*

_____ *Techniques and tips are part of the effective teacher's repertoire but in themselves will not deliver effective teaching and learning.*

_____ *Through reading, observation, discussion and practice your skills will develop.*

_____ *Students will occasionally exhibit really challenging behaviours and as a trainee you need to be confident to use not only your skills but also to call on the support of the school's staff and procedures.*

Further reading

Blum, P. (2001) *A Teacher's Guide to Anger Management*. London. RoutledgeFalmer. This book offers a range of tips, techniques and strategies and is written by a successful practitioner.

Cowley, S. (2001) *Getting the Buggers to Behave*. London. Continuum. This book is a bestseller and attracted considerable attention when it received a very positive endorsement from Tim Brighouse. It has spawned a series of books for teachers.

MacGrath, M. (1998) *The Art of Teaching Peacefully*. London. David Fulton.

Marland, M. (1975) *The Craft of the Classroom*. London. Heinemann Educational Books. This book is a very accessible and practical survival guide with ideas which are still applicable today. A new edition is in preparation.

Rogers, B. (1997) *You Know the Fair Rule*. London. Prentice Hall. This book contains lots of good advice and strategies for making management easier and also good fun.

Watkins, C. and Wagner, P. (2000) *Improving School Behaviour*. London. Paul Chapman. This book is based on detailed research and offers insights and ideas in a very readable style.

For further information on managing behaviour for learning, visit **www.learning matters.co.uk/education/learnteach/chapt5.html**

6 TEACHING LITERACY ACROSS THE CURRICULUM

ROB BATHO

Professional Standards for QTS

 2.1c, 3.3.2c

To be awarded QTS to teach a subject at Key Stage 3, you must know and understand the cross-curricular expectations of the National Curriculum and be familiar with the guidance set out in the National Strategy for Key Stage 3. You must also be able to use the cross-curricular elements, such as literacy and numeracy, set out in the National Strategy for Key Stage 3, in your teaching, as appropriate to your specialist subject.

You may find it helpful to read through the appropriate section of the handbook that accompanies the Standards for the Award of QTS for clarification and support.

Introduction

Anyone who is reading this book is likely to have sophisticated literacy skills but may not know how they acquired them or be able to identify them in order to teach them to others. This lack of understanding is not unusual and is not confined to literacy. Think of riding a bike or swimming. Imagine how difficult it would be to explain how to do one of those activities, for which you have tacit understanding, to someone who hasn't a clue. Part of the difficulty is remembering how you acquired those skills in the first place. More than likely you would have had some tuition and, most importantly, support and advice as you practised, spluttered or wobbled your way to success. To attempt to achieve such success and learn those skills only through trial and error and immersion in experience, without tuition, guidance or support can often lead to failure and an unwillingness in the learner to try again. The same can be said for literacy; all of its skills can be taught and can lead to more effective and efficient learning. As a good reader yourself (and probably writer and speaker too), you may not realise how important it is for weaker readers to be taught and given support in developing their reading skills and strategies, and that the same applies to writing and speaking and listening.

The purpose of this chapter on literacy across the curriculum is to encourage you, as a beginning teacher, to be alert to the specific literacy demands and skills of your subject so that you are in a position to support students in your class to develop their own literacy skills and by so doing improve their ability to understand your subject and to communicate that understanding to others.

The chapter will consider briefly the nature of and the context and reasons for literacy across the curriculum in secondary schools before focusing on strategies, supported by evidence from research, which can assist teachers in improving the literacy skills of students in all subjects. It will also offer practical tasks to help improve your understanding of literacy within the school context, and finally, summarise the key points of the chapter and suggests further reading.

The context

In 1998 the National Literacy Strategy and the National Numeracy Strategy were introduced to improve standards of literacy and numeracy in primary schools. These initiatives were built on and developed into the Key Stage 3 National Strategy with the introduction of the English and mathematics strands in 2001 and science, foundation subjects, ICT and behaviour and attendance in subsequent years. Literacy is one of the cross-curricular elements of the Key Stage 3 National Strategy.

The need to improve literacy in schools arose out of evidence indicating poor standards of literacy in England and Wales. For example, the DfEE report *A Fresh Start* (1999) reports that:

- **an estimated seven million adults in England cannot locate the page reference for plumbers in the *Yellow Pages;***
- **of the 12 OEDC nations surveyed in 1997 for levels of adult literacy, only Poland and Ireland emerged with a lower level than Britain.**

Look at the Professional Standards for QTS at the beginning of this chapter. Those 'cross-curricular expectations' refer to numeracy and ICT as well as to literacy, and the expectations for literacy are discussed below. The guidance in the Key Stage Strategy which is referred to can be found in the Key Stage 3 Strategy *Framework for Teaching English* (DfEE 2001a) and some of it will be considered later in this chapter. But what is also being clearly stated in the two Standards quoted is that it isn't sufficient for you to simply know and understand the cross-curricular expectations but that you demonstrate through your teaching that you can teach aspects of literacy as befits the literacy demands of your specialist subject.

What is literacy?

Before going any further, it is important to define the boundaries of what is meant by *literacy* in the context of literacy across the curriculum. Until the latter part of the twentieth century, literacy was defined as simply reading and writing, but since the late 1980s it has been argued (Graff 1987, Meek 1991, Cairney 1995) that there is a plurality of literacies which includes such areas of knowledge as the visual arts and the media. Whilst accepting that argument, in this chapter literacy is defined as reading, writing and speaking and listening to maintain parity with the National Curriculum (DfEE/QCA 2000) and the Key Stage 3 Strategy *Framework for the Teaching of English* (DFEE 2001a). Moreover, David Wray (2001), when writing about literacy in the secondary curriculum, gives a definition of literacy which suits the purpose of this chapter:

Literacy is the ability to read and use written information and to write appropriately for a range of purposes. It also involves the integration of speaking, listening and critical thinking with reading and writing and includes the knowledge which enables a speaker, reader or writer to recognise and use language appropriate to different social occasions

(Wray 2001, p. 12).

Literacy is not being viewed as a mere set of basic, functional skills to meet societal demands such as filling in forms or reading newspaper headlines, it is rather seen as a means to enable individuals to apply their literacy skills, knowledge and strategies to a range of texts and situations, and, as Eve Bearne (1999, p. 202) puts it, 'being able to read the small print as well as read between the lines'.

Literacy and subjects

The view that language and literacy are the responsibility of all subject teachers is one which is advocated in the expectations of the National Curriculum:

Pupils should be taught in all subjects to express themselves correctly and appropriately and to read accurately and with understanding.

Pupils should be taught the technical and specialist vocabulary of subjects and how to use and spell these words. They should also be taught to use the patterns of language vital to understanding and expression in different subjects. These include the construction of sentences, paragraphs and texts that are often used in a subject.

(DfEE/QCA 2000, p. 40)

In the Rationale to the *Framework for Teaching English* (DfEE 2001a), literacy and language are also viewed as the responsibility of all subject areas:

Language is the principal medium of learning in a school, and every teacher needs to cultivate it as a tool for learning. Teachers have a genuine stake in strong language skills because language enables thought.

(DfEE 2001, p.15)

It will make more sense to students if they consider specific literacy matters within the context of the subject where it naturally occurs (e.g. a science report in science, an historical enquiry in history). Each subject, in the way it is structured and formulated, will make certain and specific literacy demands on students beyond some that may be common to most or all subjects (and which the English department may well attend to). As Christine Counsell (2001) explains:

A subject ... is a way of working with certain kinds of information in order to answer certain kinds of questions. A subject is not 'information'; it is knowledge. Any knowledge has a structure ... The way a subject uses words, sentences and texts will be dominated not just by its types of information but by the questions and issues that each subject confronts.

(Counsell 2001)

Sheeran and Barnes (1991), when discussing writing in subject areas, take much the same view:

> Cognitive and communicative ground rules are the essential definers of any discipline … Specialist subjects consist of both implicit and explicit rules and organising principles governing both academic cognition and the social presentation of knowledge in the form of writing.
>
> (Sheeran and Barnes 1991, pp. 55 and 101)

The Qualifications and Curriculum Authority (QCA 2001) in their publication *Language at Work in Lessons: Literacy Across the Curriculum at Key Stage 3*, underline the importance of all subject teachers being in involved in language work because teachers who currently incorporate a focus for language in their subject believe that it will:

- **help pupils manage their learning in a subject more confidently and effectively;**
- **enable pupils to make good progress with the subject's increasing conceptual complexity and the specialist language involved;**
- **give pupils the tools to articulate, explain and justify their ideas and understanding;**
- **enhance pupils' achievements overall.**

(QCA 2001, p. 5)

Having established the need for literacy teaching in all subjects, what then of the approaches and strategies which you could adopt to assist students' literacy development?

Approaches and strategies for teaching literacy across the curriculum

Research suggests that there are many such strategies and there is not the space here to detail them all. Neither is it the intention to consider separately reading, writing and speaking and listening, mainly because a number of the strategies require all four aspects of literacy to combine in support of each other. For instance, speaking and listening are essential to the discussion of reading and the sharing and planning of writing; and writing a specific text type for the first time is best promoted through the initial exploration through reading of the conventions and patterns of such a text. However, what can be done is to approach and group the strategies in a way that should help teachers who are planning for literacy in their lessons. The approach to be adopted is an active one. It will also be expressed chronologically in terms of the cyclical sequence for teaching from the planning stage, through the lesson introduction, the main part of the lesson, the plenary and the ensuing evaluation and assessment which feeds back into future planning (see Figure 1).

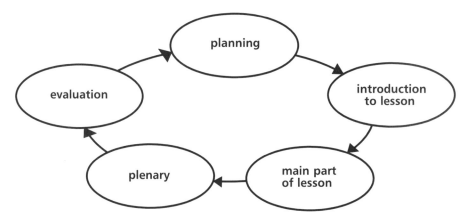

Figure 1: The teaching cycle.

Wray (2001), when discussing literacy in relation to teaching and learning, makes the point that:

> It is useful for secondary teachers to recognise that many of the processes involved in supporting literacy are also involved in developing learning.
>
> (Wray 2001, p. 50)

Planning

In planning for literacy, you first of all need to identify and select which aspect of literacy needs developing, and in many subject department schemes or units of work that selection will already have been done, very often where the objectives for learning have been adapted or taken from the Key Stage 3 Strategy *Framework for the Teaching of English* (DFEE 2001a). Departments might also have adapted their schemes of work to include literacy using the QCA's schemes of work in combination with their publications *Language for Learning* (QCA 2000) and *Language at Work in Lessons* (QCA 2001) which demonstrate, through worked examples, how literacy objectives (taken from the Strategy's *Framework*) can be employed effectively in planning and classroom practice. Once the literacy objective has been identified, then you can consider the strategies which you think will most help students meet that objective in the lesson. That range of strategies will be explored in the sections to follow.

Practical task

Think of a Year 7, 8 or 9 lesson in your subject which you have recently seen taught, and ask yourself what was the main literacy demand of that lesson. Did it concern reading, writing or speaking and listening? Find a copy of the **Framework for the Teaching of English** *(DfEE 2001a) and identify an objective for that year and for that aspect of literacy. Jot it down together with ideas for how that objective could have been addressed in the lesson in order to assist students' competence with that aspect of literacy. You might then like to share your ideas with your subject mentor or tutor.*

Lesson introduction

During the introduction you should clearly state and explain to students what the *literacy objective* for the lesson is in order that they can know what is to be expected of them. Wray (2001) emphasises the importance of teachers setting clear literacy objectives in contributing to high quality teaching:

> High quality teaching can be characterised by several factors, one of which is clarity of purpose. Making the literacy objective of a lesson explicit helps do this.
>
> (Wray 2001, p. 50)

A further strategy which is often introduced at this stage, but which should also precede most tasks, whether they be to do with literacy or not, is the *activation of prior knowledge*. Langer (1981), following her development of a method for identifying and classifying prior knowledge in students, found that, when reading, those students who engaged in activating their prior knowledge learned and retained more than those who did not. She argued that activating prior knowledge helps students make new learning more meaningful. Activating prior knowledge can provide students with a bridge between their existing knowledge and the new and it can also assist the teacher in early assessment of students' knowledge as a basis for further planning. If this activation does not happen then, as Wray (1999) points out, learning is: 'rote only, and is soon forgotten once deliberate attempts to remember it have stopped' (p. 54). Practical activities which activate prior knowledge can range straightforwardly from you asking the students what they know, to the following:

- **brainstorming around the subject to be focused on;**
- **predicting what might happen next building on previous knowledge and/or experience;**
- **word association from key word, picture or artefact from the subject to be focused on;**
- **filling in a mind-map, or grids (further details later).**

Main part of the lesson

What is important in the main part of the lesson is that wherever possible it should be directly and explicitly linked to the introduction. The teaching process should generally follow a movement which begins with teacher explication and demonstration to the whole class, through a series of activities which are often collaborative to support students' learning, to students working independently. This teaching process owes much to the ideas of Vygotsky (1962) who suggested that learners learn best when they start learning with an expert (could be teacher, parent, other adult or peer), who they first watch and observe, before gradually, under the guiding hand and eye of the expert, they take over some parts of the work, and then as confidence and competence grows, they take over more and more until they finally take over the task completely and work unaided. Lewis and Wray (2000), in their work on literacy in the secondary school, have translated this process into four distinct stages.

1. Demonstration.
2. Joint activity.

3. Supported activity.
4. Individual activity.

DEMONSTRATION

Particularly if this task is to involve a new type of writing or the reading of a text not met before, it often helps students if you speak aloud your thoughts so that they can gain an insight into the mental processes. Bereiter and Scardamalia (1987), who researched the writing process and composition, emphasise the importance of the teacher modelling writing composition:

> The thinking that goes on in composition needs to be modelled by the teacher, who can thereby show the problem-solving and planning processes that … pupils are often unaware of … and so that they can benefit from observing and discussing each other's mental efforts.
>
> (Bereiter and Scardmalia 1987, p. 174)

Similarly when students are expected to read an unfamiliar text (a subject text book, a reference text [which could be electronic], a pamphlet etc) you could use an enlarged version (via OHT) of part of the text and demonstrate the reading skills needed.

Practical task

WRITING NON-FICTION

To explore this idea of using an unfamiliar text, find a piece of non-fiction writing connected with your subject (it could be a chapter from a book, a magazine article, a leaflet etc) which you could use with your students. Now, using the Literacy Across the Curriculum training folder (DfEE 2001b) turn to page 9 in the unit on Writing Non-Fiction, and try to identify first of all the category (e.g. recount, explanation etc) that your piece best fits. Following that, use the Conventions grid on page 10 and attempt to describe the main conventions of your piece, and then compare your suggestions with those for your category which are given in Handout 2.4 at the end of that section.

JOINT ACTIVITY

This is where, 'The expert and the learner share the activity' (Lewis and Wray 2000, p. 27), and in terms of the writing and reading activities referred to above, it could be where, having demonstrated the writing of the first couple of sentences of a type of writing, you ask students to suggest the next sentence or so and discuss the suggestions as you write them on the board. Or, with reading, having demonstrated certain skills, you ask students to offer their readings.

SUPPORTED ACTIVITY

In this stage of the process you, the teacher as expert, should maintain careful observation of the students and a readiness to assist but ask the students to work on the activity, sometimes with a partner or as part of a small group or with other support (writing frames, diagrams, instructions etc). It can also be the stage, again for reading or writing, where you work closely with one particular group of students in order to support and monitor their progress.

Practical task

GROUP TALK
Think back over some lessons you have observed recently and jot down the different types of student groupings (paired, small group [4-6], large group [6+], mixed ability etc) you observed. How were the groups organised? What would you say was the function and purpose of such groupings? Now look through the Management of Group Talk section of the Literacy Across the Curriculum training folder (DfEE 2001b) and compare your responses, focusing particularly on 7.2 Choosing the size and composition of groups, 7.4 Strategies for organising group talk and 7.8 Golden rules.

INDIVIDUAL ACTIVITY
Some students may attain this stage earlier than others. You need to be sensitive to students' progress and needs in the early stages of support.

Plenary

For more information on multiple intelligences, see Chapter 2, p. 29.

The plenary is a vital stage in the lesson. It is the point where you and the students can reflect upon, review and consolidate what has been learnt so far; a point where the learning objectives for literacy, stated at the opening of the lesson, can be revisited. This is a time which can develop a student's metacognitive intelligence (one of seven different intelligences identified by Howard Gardner [1993]), the ability to reflect upon and take control of one's learning.

Evaluation and assessment

This is another important area, where you need to both evaluate the effectiveness of the lesson on students' literacy development in order to inform future lesson planning, and to assess individual students' literacy learning so that class and individual literacy targets can be reviewed and set. You can achieve this informally, during (through talking with, listening to and observing students) and after the lesson (through reading and marking students' work).

A word or two on marking written work for literacy. When you set a piece of written work, indicate which aspects of literacy will be commented on or 'marked'. This requires you to prioritise and be selective. For example, if one of the objectives for the lesson has been to learn and spell key vocabulary, it would be appropriate to tell students that those key words will be assessed both for understanding and spelling (rather than marking every spelling mistake). Similarly, if the literacy objective had been understanding how to introduce paragraphs in a particular type of writing in a subject, comments on the success or otherwise of the paragraph opening would also be appropriate. An important element to consider when responding to students' work is that of praise and positive reinforcement. On this subject, Lewis and Wray

(2001, p. 51) make the point that low levels of literacy are often associated with poor self-esteem and advocate teachers giving positive rather than negative feedback to students on their reading, writing and speaking and listening. Debra Myhill in her book *Better Writing* (2001), which is based on the research she carried out into writing in schools, gives the advice to teachers when assessing writing to 'isolate and praise what is effective as well as weaknesses' (p. 98).

The EXIT model and further strategies

The EXIT model

The EXIT model (Extending Interactions with Texts) grew out of the work of David Wray and Maureen Lewis on the Nuffield Extending Literacy (EXEL) Project. The purpose of the EXIT model was to present a 'description of the processes involved in learning with texts' (Lewis and Wray 2000) and thereby to suggest certain strategies which are directly linked to the model. Lewis and Wray identified ten mental activities involved in learning with texts and devised a ten-stage process as follows:

1. Elicitation of previous knowledge.
2. Establishing purposes.
3. Locating information.
4. Adopting an appropriate strategy.
5. Interacting with text.
6. Monitoring understanding.
7. Making a record.
8. Evaluating information.
9. Assisting memory.
10. Communicating information.

(Lewis and Wray 2000)

As can be seen, the sequence complements in part the sequence for teaching from the earlier part of this chapter, with its allusions to activating prior knowledge, stating the learning objective and evaluating the learning. Each part of the sequence can be linked to certain strategies. As mentioned earlier, there are far too many to be listed here but it is worth referring to a few.

One particularly effective group of strategies which would appear within 'Interacting with text' in Lewis and Wray's EXIT model and which has been in use in schools for many years is termed DARTS.

DARTS

DARTS stands for Directed Activities Related to Texts and they were activities first devised in 1984 by Lunzer and Gardner to further and encourage active approaches to reading. Since DARTS inception, teachers have added to and amended activities, but helpfully, Geoff Dean (2000, pp. 110-111), following many others, has categorised them into:

- **reconstructive activities;**
- **processing activities.**

With reconstructive activities, the text has been altered in some way and the students have to reconstruct it and it includes such activities as cloze procedure which involves students filling in words which have been deleted from a text; sequencing, where the text has been cut up into segments and the students have to reorganise them and give a reason for their decisions; or prediction, where students are given a text where the ending of it or the ending of a section is missing and they have to predict the next part based upon their reading and understanding of their reading so far.

Processing activities require the students to work with unamended texts and include such activities as text marking, where students are asked to apply a specific focus or question to the text and to respond by highlighting or annotating the parts of the text that refer to the focus or question; and questioning, where they are asked to generate questions about the text being studied for others to attempt to answer.

Most DARTS activities lend themselves to collaborative work, where students work in pairs or groups, and can be seen as especially useful in supported activity in the main part of a lesson.

Another effective strategy for use with texts can be the use of grids to help in terms of activating prior knowledge, establishing a purpose and making a record. Lewis and Wray advocate the use of two in particular: the KWL grid and the QUADS grid (Lewis and Wray 2000).

KWL GRID

What do I *know* about this topic?	What do I *want* to know about it?	What have I *learnt* about it?

It can be seen that this grid helps the students to organise their approach and to record their findings and is based on 'three cognitive steps – accessing prior knowledge, determining what needs to be learnt, recalling what has been learnt'. (Lewis and Wray 2000).

QUADS GRID

Question	Answer	Details	Source

This grid acts in a similar way to the KWL without so much emphasis on the activation of prior knowledge but with more emphasis on recording information. Students are required initially to formulate a question about the topic they are exploring, to find (via books, internet etc.) and record the answer, but also to record any relevant details connected with their research question as well as the source of the information.

Writing frames

It was through the EXIT project that Lewis and Wray suggested that the use of 'frames' could act as a support for students when they are engaged in writing (particularly non-fiction) in any subject. A 'frame' in this context is simply a bare outline of a text such as the one below (Figure 2: Lewis and Wray 2000, p. 93):

UK and Kenya – a comparison

Although .... and .... are different they are alike in some interesting ways.

For example they both ....

....

They are also similar in ....

....

They also have the same ....

....

Finally they both ....

....

Figure 2: Example of a writing frame.

Writing frames are helpful in structuring text, providing examples of ways to begin both whole texts and paragraphs and how to connect the different parts of a text, but, as Roger Beard points out:

> they are intended to be used as a kind of prompt, eventually to be dispensed with, as children begin to adopt the features of the genre for themselves.
>
> (Beard 2000, p. 113)

Spelling

The ability to spell is not innate; it is a skill which can be learned. There are various strategies which can be employed to help students improve their spelling. It is first of all important to recognise that there are three basic reasons why students may be poor at spelling.

1. They have underdeveloped visual memory – they can't remember how words look.
2. They have underdeveloped auditory analysis – they have poor awareness of the constituent sounds of words (phonological awareness).
3. They have underdeveloped intellectual awareness – they lack the understanding or

ability to use knowledge of the way words are derived or structured or follow spelling conventions.

It follows that the spelling strategies which you advocate for your students (individual and whole class) should attempt to address these weaknesses singularly or together as does the popular 'look – cover – say – write – check' method.

Make spelling active. When a student asks you for a spelling, you should resist the temptation to give the spelling immediately but instead ask the student to try spelling it.

Classroom story

In Jane Marston's science class one student, Alex, put up his hand and asked her how to spell immediately. Jane asked Alex to try spelling it.
'I-M-E-D-I-A-T-E-L-Y,' Alex uttered.
'Very good, Alex,' responded the teacher, 'You have ten out of the eleven letters right. There's one missing; what d'you think it might be?'
'Is it another M, Miss?'
'It is Alex, well done.'

The lesson in this story is that even if the student doesn't get the whole word right you should praise them for the number of letters they do get right before asking them or indicating where the error lies. You should ask the class how to spell words which are vital to the subject they are addressing in the lesson, and you should encourage students to keep a spelling log book which contains words which are important in their subject and which they can easily refer to.

Practical task

VOCABULARY

Find out and make a list of the key vocabulary for your subject in Year 7 and see how you might incorporate some of those words into a scheme of work for that year.

Using the teaching environment to support literacy

Medwell (Medwell et al. 1998 in Lewis and Wray 2001, p. 49), in the *Effective Teachers of Literacy* project, found that it was important to create 'literate environments' in the classroom. It is yet another way for the teachers in the school to show how valued literacy is in that community. The teaching environment could be any site in the secondary school where teaching and learning takes place including classrooms, IT suites, gymnasia and drama studios, but also, other sites such as the school's entrance hall and corridors. All are sites which teachers could use to support and emphasise literacy within and across subjects. You, as an individual subject teacher, could ensure for instance that wall displays are changed regularly to coincide with current literacy objectives for different classes (e.g. key terminology and vocabulary); or that good examples of students' writing are displayed attractively and effectively; that key books are displayed and that literacy materials and resources such as dictionaries are easily accessible by students.

Practical task

LITERACY WALK

During a break, take a walk around the school and look to see how the school environment (classrooms, corridors, reception areas, halls etc) supports students' literacy development. Make a note of good examples and practice in your school and be prepared to share it with others. For example:

- *in which areas are there examples of advice for students as to how to improve an aspect of their literacy?*
- *in which areas are there good displays of books?*
- *in which areas are there good displays of recent students' written work?*

Literacy and students with English as an Additional Language (EAL)

The inclusion of students learning English as an additional language is a key principle of the National Curriculum 2000. Literacy competence and confidence is essential for students with EAL if they are to access all subjects in the curriculum. Virtually all of the strategies for developing literacy outlined above will be helpful to those students because they encourage teacher support, scaffolded activities, collaborative working, the activation of prior knowledge and planning for talk. In order to be of greatest assistance to their students you will, in addition, need to know the language and literacy background and identity as well as the previous educational experiences of your students. You should also have high expectations of your students and plan for them all to be involved.

Literacy across the curriculum and the role of the English teacher

If your subject is English, all that has been discussed so far in terms of strategies and approaches will apply to your classroom practice, but it is not your responsibility to teach all aspects of literacy that will be covered across the curriculum. I hope that it is now clear that each subject has a responsibility for identifying its own literacy demands and teaching those accordingly. With English as your subject, what you can do to help support literacy across the curriculum is to teach some of those generic aspects of literacy which will support students' literacy in other subjects. For instance you can teach pupils many of the conventions of English spelling; strategies for spelling; paragraphing; punctuation; understanding and writing the main text types; reading strategies; the roles and skills of group discussion etc.

Teaching literacy across the curriculum:

a summary of key points

The foregrounding and teaching of literacy is an essential responsibility of all teachers, whatever their subject, if they are to fully develop and sustain the learning of all their students. The following are, I believe, the key points from the chapter which will lead to your success in improving the literacy skills of the students you teach.

- *Understand the literacy demands of your subject.*
- *Plan your lessons to include literacy objectives and the development of students' literacy.*
- *Teach literacy skills. Don't assume that their literacy will automatically improve by simply doing more reading or writing.*
- *Model and demonstrate good literacy practice.*
- *Provide support and guidance for students' reading, writing and speaking and listening.*
- *Respond constructively to students' literacy in their reading, writing and speaking and listening.*

Further reading

DfEE (2001a) *Framework for Teaching English: Years 7, 8 and 9.* London. DfEE. The document which contains all of the objectives for literacy for Key Stage 3 as well as advice on planning and guidance on inclusion.

DfEE (2001b) *Literacy Across the Curriculum.* London. DfEE. This is the training folder for all subjects at Key Stage 3 and it contains discussions and teaching advice on all aspects of literacy from writing non-fiction to spelling and from active reading to managing group talk.

DfES (2002, 2004) *Literacy in …* series. A series of booklets and video extracts exmplifying good practice in literacy teaching in art, PE, MFL, design and technology, history, geography, music, RE, citizenship and careers.

Lewis M. and Wray D. (2000) *Literacy in the Secondary School.* London. David Fulton. This contains information on the EXEL project together with discussion and advice on teaching strategies to improve students' literacy.

Myhill, D. (2001) *Better Writing.* Westley. Courseware Publications. Good advice on teaching writing based on recent research.

QCA (2000) *Language for Learning in Key Stage 3.* London. QCA. Useful advice on mapping the objectives in the QCA schemes of work for various subjects.

Website

www.standards.dfes.gov.uk/keystage3/ This site contains materials for literacy across the curriculum (look in 'Publications') as well as other material relating to the Key Stage 3 National Strategy.

For further information on teaching literacy across the curriculum, visit **www.learningmatters.co.uk/education/learnteach/chapt6.html**

Professional Standards for QTS

 2.1c, 3.3.2c

To be awarded QTS to teach a subject at Key Stage 3, you need to be familiar with the cross-curricular expectations and guidance contained in the National Curriculum and the National Strategy for Key Stage 3. You also need to be able to incorporate these expectations for numeracy into your teaching of your specialist subject.

You may find it helpful to read through the appropriate section of the handbook that accompanies the Standards for the award of QTS for clarification and support.

Introduction

In this chapter, the following questions will be considered.

- **What is numeracy?**
- **Why focus on numeracy across the curriculum?**
- **What are the objectives of numeracy across the curriculum?**
- **What maths is relevant to your specialist subject?**
- **How can you make sure you know the maths you need?**
- **How can you plan to incorporate numeracy in your lessons?**
- **What's important in delivering such a lesson?**

You will require access to three DfES publications:

- *Key Stage 3 National Strategy Framework for Teaching Mathematics: Years 7, 8 and 9* (referred to as the **Framework** in the remainder of this chapter);
- *Numeracy Across the Curriculum Notes for School-based Training* (referred to as the **NAC notes**);
- the video from *Numeracy Across the Curriculum Support Materials for School-based Training*.

These should be available through your training provider and are widely available in secondary schools.

What is numeracy?

Numeracy is not just about being able to do calculations: it is about being able to use mathematics effectively outside the mathematics classroom. This includes for example the ability to use simple formulae, understand basic probability and create and interpret graphs. A detailed definition is given on page 9 of the Framework.

It is probably more useful to think of numeracy skills as being mathematical skills used in a real context rather than as a particular group of mathematical skills, as it can be argued that numeracy encompasses all of the mathematics at KS3 (Perks and Prestage 2001).

Why focus on numeracy across the curriculum?

Do you feel bogged down at the thought of including numeracy in your subject teaching? Surely teacher training is tough enough without throwing maths into it!

Practical task

Spend 20 minutes writing a response or drawing a picture about how you feel about mathematics. Do you enjoy it? Have you found it hard? Boring? How confident are you with everyday maths? Compare your notes with two other people (preferably fellow trainees), one of whom is confident about maths and one of whom is not, and look at the cartoon in appendix 1 of the NAC notes.

You have probably just pinpointed a major problem with numeracy: many people dislike maths, become anxious when required to do any maths and lack confidence in their ability. Many people also have very negative images of mathematicians and these likewise (and perhaps particularly for girls) can get in the way of learning. Here are some common beliefs that just aren't true:

- maths doesn't involve creativity;
- maths is about rules to be memorised;
- boys are better at maths than girls;
- some people can do maths but some can't.

Also, being 'innumerate' is socially acceptable in a way that being 'illiterate' isn't. Hence there can be little incentive to become competent at mathematics.

Does this matter? I get very anxious about the idea of diving off a board 20 feet above the water and hence I avoid having to do it and have not developed the skills needed to do it successfully. Impact on my life? Negligible.

The effects of maths avoidance and lack of skill are not negligible. Mathematical skills are increasingly needed in employment: research has shown that poor numeracy skills have more impact on employment prospects than poor literacy skills (Basic Skills Agency 1997).

This research, together with the relatively poor performance of English students in an international study of mathematics achievement in 1995, led to the introduction of the National Numeracy Strategy at KS1/KS2 in 1998 and at KS3 in 2001. This has required a change in teaching strategies in mathematics, with an emphasis on direct instruction and whole-class teaching involving a high proportion of oral and mental work. A detailed programme of study for mathematics for each year from Year I to Year 9 has also been introduced.

The Numeracy across the Curriculum initiative

Another aspect of the Strategy is the Numeracy across the Curriculum initiative, initiated in secondary schools in 2001. In the past, most departments have worked in isolation, meeting the numeracy demands of their own subject in a piecemeal way with no reference to what students are learning in mathematics. It is a commonplace observation that students do not seem to be able to use what they have learned in mathematics in other subjects: a science teacher, when asked about the chief issues in numeracy in science replied 'they don't know anything'. She, like many other teachers, taught the maths that her students needed to know as and when they needed it for science. Research has shown that this is because learning always takes place in a particular context and does not readily transfer to other contexts (Lave 1988). Hence students may well be able to draw graphs in mathematics classrooms – but can't draw the same graphs in science classrooms. The links between contexts need to be made explicit to students for any transfer of learning to occur. For this to happen, mathematics and subject departments need to work in close collaboration to achieve consistency in approaches and expectations: enabling this collaboration to take place is a main aim of the initiative.

Practical task

Watch the excerpts from a geography lesson and a history lesson contained in the NAC video. In what ways have the students been prepared for these lessons in their mathematics lessons? How do the students benefit, in geography, history and mathematics, by the collaboration that has taken place?

What are the objectives of Numeracy across the Curriculum?

The fundamental objective is that standards in numeracy will be raised and that learning in other subjects will be enhanced. A full list of numeracy objectives is given in the handout Numeracy across the Curriculum Objectives available with the NAC notes. This contains a breakdown by year of the objectives given on page 9 of the Framework. These priorities have been identified:

- **to improve accuracy, particularly in calculation, measurement and graphical work;**
- **to improve interpretation and presentation of graphs, charts and diagrams;**
- **to improve reasoning and problem-solving.**

In order to achieve these objectives, schools will have designated a numeracy co-ordinator and ideally, the curriculum for mathematics and other subjects will have begun to be organised so that topics required for other subjects are first taught by the mathematics department. Schools should also be developing a numeracy policy which:

- **sets out an agreed approach to:**
  the teaching of agreed numeracy skills;
  vocabulary, notation and units to be used;
  use of calculators and other ICT;
  methods for calculation;
  algebraic techniques;
  the representation of graphs;
- **indicates areas of collaboration between subjects and processes for facilitating collaboration;**
- **gives links with using and applying mathematics;**
- **gives advice from the mathematics department on common difficulties, errors and misconceptions.**

At the time of writing, however, this is a new initiative: it is not expected that all of its aims will be achieved immediately. In particular, collaboration between different subject groups is expected to be an ongoing process.

Practical task

Find out from the numeracy co-ordinator in your school how the Numeracy across the Curriculum initiative is being implemented.

What maths is relevant to your specialist subject?

The maths necessary to different subjects will vary: geography, science and design technology rely on mathematics extensively (for example can you imagine design technology without measurement, or science and geography without graphs?), whereas there are no specific demands for mathematical skills in studying English.

Mathematics which is not strictly required can also be used to enrich subject teaching. A good example is found in the excerpt from the history lesson on the NAC video, where pie charts are used to enhance student learning about the daily life of a monk.

Here are some further enrichment examples from English and MFL:

- **Exploring the metrical pattern of poetry when using a poem as a model for writing.**
- **Exploring average sentence length in samples of a newspaper's front page over time and considering whether any generalisations can be made.**
- **Number games such as Countdown conducted in the target language.**

- Looking at the structure of the number system via the different words used for number in different languages.
- Money: conversations around shopping and Internet 'shopping', currency conversions.
- Conducting surveys and presenting data in the target language, interpreting data from the target language country.
- Using mathematical language (e.g. square, rectangular) in describing objects.

Practical task

Identify the mathematical content necessary to your subject and begin to identify areas where maths could enrich your subject. Some sources of information are listed below:

- *the QCA schemes of work (and teacher's guide) for your subject;*
- *your subject department;*
- *page 23 of the Framework;*
- *'Learning across the Curriculum' at www.nc.uk.net/learn.html (search on application of number);*
- *the Mathematics Association publication Numeracy across the Curriculum;*
- *unit 3 of the NAC;*
- *a search on the Internet on your subject and mathematics.*

As well as identifying mathematics content (such as percentages), improving reasoning and problem-solving will require you to identify the relationship between your subject and mathematical thinking skills (which are the sorts of skills you used in creating maths GCSE coursework). Thinking skills in mathematics in the National Curriculum are known as 'using and applying' and are categorised as:

- problem-solving (making decisions about problems and methods and monitoring decision-making);
- communication (formulating, discussing, interpreting and presenting findings);
- reasoning (finding solutions and giving justifications).

Pages 20 to 22 in the Framework give a description of the generic thinking skills in mathematics: you may find it useful to read these pages, identify how these relate to the numeracy priorities and compare with thinking skills in your subject.

Many activities will focus around handling data which involves all three of the NAC priorities and also gives your students the chance to become researchers in your subject. Unit 7 in the NAC notes gives an extensive number of ideas for handling data across the curriculum.

How can you make sure you know the maths you need?

As you explore this, it's useful to keep notes of any difficulties that you encounter: students are likely to have similar difficulties!

Misconceptions in maths are common: even if you feel confident about mathematics you may find you have some. It's very important that you don't pass these on to students.

All of the statements below are true – some may surprise you! Look up the meaning of any unfamiliar mathematical words in the mathematics glossary on the QCA website at **www.qca.org.uk**

- **Multiplying doesn't always make numbers bigger.**
- **Putting a nought on the end of a number to multiply it by ten doesn't always work.**
- **Sometimes adding two numbers can give a bigger result than multiplying them.**
- **To convert square metres to square centimetres you don't multiply by 100.**
- **If the price of an item is increased by five per cent and then reduced by five per cent the final price will not be the same as the original price.**
- **On the other hand, if the price of an item is reduced by a certain percentage and then VAT is added, the result will be the same as if the VAT is added before the price is reduced.**
- **If a set of data is grouped into five class intervals, the mean could fall into any one of the intervals.**
- **If you toss a coin twice the probability of throwing two heads is not 1/3.**
- **Two cuboids with the same volume will not always have the same surface area.**
- **If you double the lengths of a shape you will not double the area and the volume.**
- **Division sometimes makes numbers larger.**
- **When the area of a shape increases the perimeter can sometimes decrease.**
- **Dividing any number by zero does not give zero.**
- **The order in which you combine numbers using +, −, × or ÷ sometimes matters.**
- **There are nine times as many students as teachers in a school. P represents the number of students and T represents the number of teachers in the school. Hence 9T = P.**   (Adapted from Pope and Sharma 2001)

Detailed explanations of a variety of misconceptions may be found at **www.ex. ac.uk/cimt/help/**

Now for the mathematical skills involved. The following task may be time-consuming, but it will:

- **deepen your understanding of the numeracy objectives;**
- **enable you to identify your own strengths and weaknesses;**
- **give you an awareness of the year in which different mathematics topics are taught and the progression between years;**
- **indicate further connections between mathematics and your own subject;**
- **enable you to see some of the connections between different aspects of mathematics (extremely important in successful numeracy teaching [Wiliam et al. 1998]);**
- **give you some excellent practice for the TTA's numeracy skills test!**

In the Supplement of Examples section of the Framework, find the examples that correspond to the various Numeracy across the Curriculum objectives and work through any that do not seem straightforward to you. Repeat this for any areas of mathematics which are necessary to your subject but not covered by the numeracy objectives. You might also want to read pages 10 to 22 of the Framework which contain an overview of the different areas of the mathematics curriculum.

One aspect of the KS3 strategy is an emphasis on skills in mental calculation. The chances are that you were not encouraged to acquire such skills at school. If, for example, you work out the cost of eight calculators at £6.98 each you probably don't multiply 6.98 x 8 but instead use some sort of shortcut, and you might feel guilty about not working it out 'properly'. Such 'shortcuts' are called strategies and are encouraged by the Numeracy Strategy. Useful examples of such strategies can be found on pages 82-111 in the Framework supplement of examples.

How can you plan to incorporate numeracy in your lessons?

Practical task

Observe a mathematics lesson, ideally one in which mathematics relevant to your subject is being taught. Make notes of the teaching strategies used, in particular the use of questioning and mental and oral work and of the students' responses. Now observe a lesson in your subject in which mathematics is used. Contrast the teaching strategies and pupil responses with those in the mathematics lesson.

1. Identify the required mathematical skills, together with relevant misconceptions and common difficulties

Be specific about what mathematics you need: for example in the geography lesson on the NAC video, students need to find the area of a particular type of trapezium: they do not need to be able to use the general formula for the area of a trapezium. The history lesson requires awareness that many students find it difficult to use a protractor correctly and that a common misconception is that angles should be measured from the edge of the protractor, rather than from the line marked 0°. Hopefully information about misconceptions and difficulties will be contained in the school numeracy policy: if not, talk to a member of the mathematics department.

2. Identify prior learning

This is quite important in mathematics teaching: you need to ensure that you are building upon mathematics with which the students feel confident. Information about what mathematics the students have been exposed to should be in the mathematics departmental schemes of work. It is also worth looking at the yearly teaching programmes in section 3 of the Framework. Mathematical exposure is not the same as mathematical learning, however: find out as much as you can about the mathematical attainment of individual students. In particular you need to identify students who have particular difficulty with maths: they may not be the same students as the ones who find your subject difficult.

3. Decide on learning objectives

You may find at this point that there is a mismatch between the mathematics required and the students' prior learning. As the Numeracy across the Curriculum initiative becomes implemented fully, the mismatch between required mathematical skills in other subjects and prior learning in mathematics should be minimised so that you do not need to ever introduce new mathematical techniques for the first time to a class: your objectives will normally involve using mathematics in the context of your subject. If the mismatch is too great, you will need to revise your plans to include mathematics which is more appropriate to the students' prior learning.

You may find it difficult to break a piece of mathematics down into measurable objectives or to see what would be an appropriate progression: here the Framework objectives, found in both the Key Objectives section and the yearly teaching programmes, may be useful. Your objectives will normally involve consolidation of mathematical skills and application of these skills within your subject. For example the history lesson on the NAC video might have included 'gain experience in simplifying fractions' and 'interpret pie charts to draw inferences about the life of a monk'.

Remember that the cross-curricular priorities focus on accuracy, interpretation and presentation and reasoning and problem-solving. Do your learning objectives relate to these priorities?

4. Decide on teaching strategies

It may be useful to read pages 6, 26 and 27 of the Framework and compare the teaching strategies suggested with those used in your subject. Most of these will be to some extent familiar to you as they are considered good practice in most subjects.

The emphasis in the Framework is on direct interactive teaching, mental and oral work and in promoting students' thinking skills. The lesson excerpts on the video give examples of these strategies. There is an emphasis on questioning: the students are never told what to do or how to do it, but are asked to reflect on their knowledge of mathematics in order to decide for themselves. Mental calculations are required and students are asked to explain how they worked out particular answers. In addition, notice that the mathematics involved is explicitly connected with the mathematics studied in mathematics lessons.

Discussion and questioning are key teaching strategies: students can be asked how they worked out their answers, whether or not their answers are reasonable and why they have chosen their methods or reached their conclusions. Students can be encouraged to discuss their strategies and share ideas.

The Framework also promotes a three-part lesson structure (see pages 28-31): in the first part of a lesson, the oral and mental starter, students might review some of the mathematics to be used later (this review will usually be necessary at some time in the lesson). The geography teacher might have reviewed the method used to calculate the area of a trapezium in this part of the lesson. The main teaching activity would include combinations of teaching input and pupil activies, as seen in the video extracts. The final plenary could include reflections on the use of mathematics within the lesson and the conclusions which the use of mathematics has enabled.

It's important to use the same approach as the maths department in dealing with specific topics. A temptation is to show the students a shortcut, as illustrated in the following story:

Classroom story

As part of their study of rivers, students in a geography lesson were converting some numbers from fractions to percentages. The teacher noticed that the students were using a variety of methods, most of which were unfamiliar to him and many of which did not seem very efficient. The teacher decided to address the class about this and said 'I know a better method for doing this – first you ... and then you ...' The students left the class feeling confused: though able to use the shortcut in that particular lesson, none of them understood why it worked or when it could be used. The consequence was, as noted in subsequent mathematics lessons, that their basic understanding of percentages deteriorated. It would have been better for the teacher to have listened to them explaining their methods.

A major consideration will be the approach you use to calculation: you need to consider whether to use mental, written or calculator methods and plan accordingly. Note that students may well be much better at mental arithmetic than you expect: by Year 7 students are expected to add and subtract two digit numbers such as 73 and 49 mentally. If students can reasonably be expected to work out calculations mentally, telling them to use a calculator may deprive them of an opportunity to practise their skills in mental calculation. On the other hand, if the required calculations are lengthy and difficult, students may lose track of the purpose of the lesson by focusing on calculation alone. See units 5 and 6 of NAC for a consideration of calculations and calculator use.

5. Decide on assessment strategies

Appropriate assessment will enable you to gauge whether or not you have met your learning objectives and will also provide feedback which enables students to improve. Much of this you will achieve through observation and questioning during the course of your lesson. It is usually not appropriate to set a series of problems (even well related to your subject) which you can tick, cross and give a mark out of 20. While you should point out and comment on issues to do with accuracy and errors in mathematical techniques much as you would point out spelling errors in student work, the focus of your assessment should be on how well the mathematics has been used in

For further informaiton on formative assessment, see Chapter 4, p. 56.

the context of your subject. It's important to remember the general research findings about formative assessment (Black and Wiliam, 1998): students make better progress if they are aware of your assessment objectives and if you give feedback only with no mark.

What's important in delivering a lesson involving numeracy?

We're going to come back to your attitude to mathematics, because at this stage it's critical. It's easy to let your dislike, lack of confidence, or prejudices show: consider the message you are giving if you get flustered when you make an arithmetic mistake, or your voice becomes more lively when you finish the maths and can get on to the 'important' stuff in your subject or you say 'Here's an easy question, so let's hear from one of the girls' (I've heard this said!). It's crucial to convey that mathematics is an important part of your subject, and an aspect of your subject that all students can participate in: remember that much of the problem with numeracy is not just lack of attainment but negative attitudes.

Classroom story

A drama teacher was working with a group to stage a play, and they were discussing how to design the set. A student, remembering maths homework in which they'd drawn scale drawings of their rooms, suggested they could make a scale drawing. Should the teacher respond with:

'No, let's do something a bit more imaginative, and anyway you can't expect me to do anything like that – I'm not a maths teacher'
'Mmm, has anyone got any other ideas?'
'Good idea. How could we start?'

Your lack of confidence with mathematics is likely to be the biggest issue. Hopefully you will have gained some confidence through ensuring that you can in fact deal with the maths and that you have planned appropriately, but you may still be fearful of making a mistake, or feel daunted that some students will be better at maths than you are.

Classroom story

A science teacher had been transposing a formula on the board, and a student pointed out that he had made a mistake. Which do you think would be the most helpful response?

'No, I haven't.'
'Oh, uh, well it was deliberate, uh, just testing you, uh – time to set the homework!'
'Yes, I might have. Let's check it through. How did you spot it – and well done!'

Many students will be better at mental arithmetic than you are: can you add and subtract two digit numbers in your head? Remember that what you have to offer is your understanding of how maths is going to enhance your subject – and let them teach you some of their strategies!

Another issue is that of creating a supportive atmosphere. All students should feel that their contribution is of value and should not worry about making mistakes. Notice that in the geography lesson when a student gives an incorrect answer the teacher indicates that it is almost right and invites other students to correct it.

Classroom story

In comparing the proportions of various pictures an art teacher asked the class for their measurements. One student gave a measurement that was, to the teacher, obviously inaccurate. Which response will be most helpful?

'No, that's wrong. Go and do it again.'
'I'm not sure that that's quite accurate. How did you get it?'

Students should also not be put under pressure to do mathematics that they find too difficult. If you see any signs of anxiety, such as a lack of response when you ask questions, or a deterioration in behaviour, it's best to back off and do something else. Talk to someone in the mathematics department about what you observed and, with their help, plan a different strategy. On the other hand it's important that students are challenged. With reflection on your experience you will begin to achieve this balance.

For the mathematics trainee

Your responsibilities with regard to numeracy across the curriculum are rather different: it's expected that almost everything that you do as a teacher will be enhancing pupil numeracy, and you will receive detailed training on teaching mathematics as required by the Key Stage 3 Strategy as part of your subject specialist work.

There are two aspects of numeracy across the curriculum which should inform your teaching, however. First, you should bring in contexts from across the curriculum and make explicit the links between mathematics and other subjects: you might for example talk about the way in which scale drawing is used in design technology in the course of a lesson. Secondly, you should help teachers of other subjects to effectively promote numeracy within their subjects: you might for example tell the design technology teacher what approach the maths department takes to scale drawing and what difficulties are experienced by students.

Practical task

Working with a group of other trainees, which includes a mathematics trainee if possible, plan a cross-curricular day to focus on the theme of enhancing numeracy across the curriculum. Plan a lesson for your subject in detail, paying attention to the requirements given above. If possible, teach and evaluate your lesson.

Teaching numeracy across the curriculum:
a summary of key points

— *Numeracy is about using maths effectively outside the maths classroom and is an important skill for all students.*

— *The Numeracy across the Curriculum initiative, part of the KS3 Strategy, is designed to improve numeracy skills across the curriculum and also enhance the teaching of other subjects through collaboration between subject departments.*

— *To incorporate numeracy in your teaching, you need to identify the mathematics involved in your subject, ensure that you have confidence in your knowledge of this maths and plan to build on students' prior knowledge and understanding of mathematics.*

— *Key teaching strategies are the use of discussion and questioning, in which students are encouraged to explain their methods and reasoning.*

— *A supportive classroom atmosphere, in which students are not afraid to make mistakes, is important.*

Further reading

Ledwick, M. (2001) *Numeracy Across the Curriculum in Secondary Schools*. Leicester. Mathematical Association. A resource to assist in the planning and implementation of this initiative.

Perks, P. and Prestage, S. (2001) *Teaching the National Numeracy Strategy at Key Stage 3*. London. David Fulton. A very useful discussion of the ways in which the KS3 numeracy strategy may be implemented.

For further information on teaching numeracy across the curriculum, visit **www.learning matters.co.uk/education/learnteach/chapt7.html**

Professional Standards for QTS

 2.5, 2.8, 3.3.2c, 3.3.10

To be awarded QTS you must know how to use ICT effectively, both to teach your subject and to support your wider professional role. You should be able to plan to use ICT as an integral part of your teaching using the National Curriculum Programmes of Study for Key Stage 3 and the relevant national frameworks and schemes of work. You must be able to use ICT effectively in your teaching setting high expectations for your students according to the National Strategy for Key Stage 3.

You may find it helpful to read through the appropriate section of the handbook that accompanies the Standards for the Award of QTS for clarification and support.

Introduction

In a new century where Information and Communication Technology (ICT) capability is prized as never before, we are duty bound to design a curriculum for all students which will allow them to be educationally 'street-wise' with today's technology. This chapter seeks to demonstrate that the use of ICT in teaching and learning can help students learn more effectively and enjoyably with the same avid concentration and commitment that they have for computer games.

In September 2000, the new orders for the National Curriculum stated that all students in England were to be given opportunities to apply and develop their ICT capability through the use of ICT tools to support their learning in all subjects (with the exception of physical education at Key Stages I and 2). It is not the intention of this chapter for the reader to feel constrained by the statutory orders of the National Curriculum or the criteria for Initial Teacher Education. Rather that through classroom examples and results from research it will demonstrate how the use of ICT can enhance and enrich the learning experience across the curriculum and form the basis for lifelong learning. Practical tasks and ideas for the use of ICT in school will enable those embarking on the teaching profession to demonstrate a developing pedagogy of ICT.

Claims

There are many claims for what ICT can do in support of teaching and learning. For example ICT can help:

- **motivate learners and raise levels of attainment;**
- **reduce the teacher's workload;**
- **link school, home and the rest of the world.**

SOME OF THE KEY RESEARCH

The research has a shorter history than other subject areas but there is growing evidence to confirm that there is a correlation between good resources, good teaching and student attainment. *Ways Forward With ICT*, Moseley et al. (1999), although a primary focused report, has some very important conclusions demonstrating that ICT contributes to teaching and learning where:

- **clear subject-focused objectives had been identified;**
- **the teacher could use the ICT to deliver those objectives;**
- **the teacher ensured that students had ICT skills that were sufficient to enable them to achieve the subject-specific objectives;**
- **students were given sufficient access to ICT to achieve learning objectives.**

The emerging findings from the ImpaCT2 report (Becta 2001), which is evaluating the impact of the National Grid for Learning (NGfL) on schools and the Secondary School of the Future Report (2001), the purpose of which was to analyse the relationship between ICT and secondary school standards, certainly supports these claims. The first three bullet points above are concerned with teaching at its best; when not meeting these standards the report shows that teachers underestimate the capability of students although the students are generally enthusiastic about using computers and they perceive using ICT as useful. Seymour Papert's book *Mindstorms* (1980) gives an account of his vision of how computers might be used in education using the Logo language as an example. His work supports that of the Swiss psychologist Jean Piaget who spent decades studying and documenting the learning processes of young children. Piaget's constructivist philosophy believes that students excel by building and constructing for themselves the specific knowledge they need, rather than having a teacher dictate numerous facts. Therefore I would suggest that ICT lessons which are largely skills-based are unlikely to meet the subject specific learning objectives.

Visit **telematics3.ex.ac.uk/erf/** for further reading.

First steps

Knowing where to start developing your own ICT capability depends very much on your own situation but personal access to modern ICT is crucial. Explore the facilities in your own institution and visit The Laptops for Teachers Initiative at **lft.ngfl. gov. uk**

For those working towards Qualified Teacher Status, you will need to demonstrate:

- **that you are a competent user of ICT and know how to use it effectively in teaching the subject for which you are qualifying to teach;**
- **that you plan for the use of ICT in your teaching;**
- **that you are able to teach the cross-curricular elements of the Key Stage 3 Strategy;**
- **that you use ICT effectively in your teaching including opportunities for key skills.**

The evidence for these competencies will come from a range of sources such as your teaching file or classroom resources. Keeping a file of the practical tasks in this chapter which are relevant to you will be further evidence that you have met the standards. The Professional Standards for the award of QTS do not specify a list of required ICT skills although there is an ICT skills test as part of gaining QTS – see **www.tta. gov.uk** and follow the links to skills tests.

As a simple base line you should ask yourself if you can:

- **word process;**
- **use a spreadsheet for simple calculations and graphing;**
- **use a database;**
- **communicate effectively using ICT;**
- **use the Internet.**

The following sites are a useful starting point for your own professional development.

- **www.brighton.ac.uk/sms/** tutorials for the main Microsoft Office applications.
- **www.netskills.ac.uk/TonicNG/cgi/sesame?tng** is an online tutorial for use of the Internet.

Practical task

Produce and use a template for lesson planning using a word processor. Email a copy as an attachment to a colleague. Visit the Teaching and Learning section of Teachernet at www.teachernet.gov.uk/TeachingandLearning Look for examples of lesson plans in your own subject area which use ICT for teaching and learning.

When is it appropriate to use ICT?

A word of warning! One of the biggest mistakes made using ICT is when its use does not support the learning, the presumption being that just because the students are using ICT its use is appropriate. It is also easy to fall into the trap of using ICT as, for example, a reward for good behaviour, 'I'll let you go onto the Internet if you finish your work', or awarding higher attainment for work that has been produced using ICT when the content is weak.

Classroom stories

A student was asked to word-process a handwritten essay so that the teacher could use it for display.

Comment – A word-processor should have been used to allow for amending and refining during the drafting stage, and additional features such as thesaurus and spell checker would have made the use of ICT an integral part of the learning.

A group of Year 10 business studies students were researching on the Internet for their coursework and were given a worksheet to write their results on.

Comment – The students should have been copying and pasting information as they found it into a word-processing package so that they could use it using ICT in subsequent activities, thus learning to share, exchange and present information in a variety of contexts. An extension to the learning could have been a discussion on the implications of copying information from web-based sources and plagiarism.

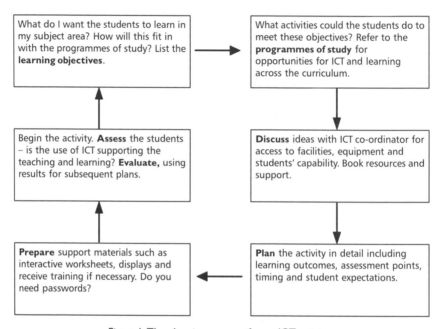

What do I want the students to learn in my subject area? How will this fit in with the programmes of study? List the **learning objectives**.

What activities could the students do to meet these objectives? Refer to the **programmes of study** for opportunities for ICT and learning across the curriculum.

Begin the activity. **Assess** the students – is the use of ICT supporting the teaching and learning? **Evaluate,** using results for subsequent plans.

Discuss ideas with ICT co-ordinator for access to facilities, equipment and students' capability. Book resources and support.

Prepare support materials such as interactive worksheets, displays and receive training if necessary. Do you need passwords?

Plan the activity in detail including learning outcomes, assessment points, timing and student expectations.

Figure 1: The planning process for an ICT activity.

Therefore it can be seen that at the planning stage the learning objectives need to be addressed in the activities, so that they can then be demonstrated in the learning outcomes.

If we look at the distinctive features of ICT we can then begin to unpack the contribution that information technology can offer within the learning environment.

The four main features are:

- **provisionality;**
- **speed and automatic functions;**
- **capacity and range;**
- **and interactivity.**

Provisionality

Work can be revised easily with ICT. For students working to extend their literacy skills or prepare a presentation this is an important feature. Word-processors can be thought processors allowing ideas to be revised without the chore of a total rewrite. A number of applications can take the tedium out of traditional methods of working and open up opportunities for higher order thinking skills and interpretation. Art and music software, for example, encourages experimentation without the fear of losing what has already been created.

Classroom story

A Year 8 history class was set the challenge of producing a newspaper front page with the start of World War One as its lead story. Initial research was done using a variety of sources (not all IT-based) and a class discussion was held in order for them to highlight the main issues. They worked in groups of about four students with each child initially as a journalist word-processing their own article and then taking on different roles such as editor. They were encouraged to use features such as double line spacing, thesaurus and spell checker for drafting, and writing frames were used to structure their arguments. The completed articles were imported into a desktop publishing package where images, graphics, etc were added with audience in mind.

www.warwick.ac.uk/staff/D.J.Wray/Ideas/frames.html

Practical task

Find an article or section of text that you want to use with your students. Consider how the use of formatting could make the text accessible for all students.

For example:

- *change the font to one such as Comic Sans – you will notice in the example that the 'a' is cursive (how students write it) and for many it is easier to read than usual print;*
- *altering font colour and size;*
- *use 'find and replace' for words which some may find difficult to understand;*
- *embolden key words.*

NB If the original text is in a book try using a scanner which can read text and import this into a word processing package. If it is web based, use copy and paste.

Speed and automatic functions

Collecting large amounts of data and processing it rapidly are tasks that computers are very good at. The graph plotting capability of spreadsheets allows students to examine quickly a number of ways of displaying data, allowing them to look for patterns without having to re-plot the data manually. Graphics and computer aided design (CAD) packages engage students with design concepts. Their ideas can be developed quickly, modelling solutions and producing sophisticated outcomes. Data logging, for example using electronic sensors, allows for higher order thinking skills as students can progress into analysis of the data rather than being involved in the tedium of collecting

For further information on formatting text for accessibility see Chapter 10, p. 134.

it. Automatic control systems can be created from a range of electronic sensors and output devices such as motors, lights and loudspeakers. As with data logging this gives immediate feedback as changes can be observed as they happen. Sense and control functions often feature strongly in design and technology, and music, but I would like to contest the notion of one area of ICT 'belonging' to a particular subject. For example, a short input on how information is processed at a supermarket check-out with credit cards and 'reward cards' as the focus would work very well in a citizenship curriculum, which is not usually associated with control technology. Students could discuss and reflect critically on the economic, legal and ethical issues associated with personal data being used to monitor shopping habits.

Practical task

Set up a spreadsheet for one or more of the classes that you teach to monitor their performance. Input test results, levels and any other data you have on the students. Use the functionality of the programme to perform tasks such exam percentages, searching for students at a particular level using graphing to compare data to predict results. Most secondary schools in England use a database called SIMS (School Information Management System), ask the SIMS manager if you can access historical data such as end of key stage results and Cognitive Ability Testing for your students. Visit www.nfer-nelson.co.uk to find more information on how you could use this data.

Classroom story

A physical education department used fitness data (bleep tests) on their students to allow them to monitor their own progress over a key stage. Students entered the data into a database and analysed their own results using increasingly complex queries. Identities were kept anonymous on the charts for the whole year group. Students began to take an increased interest in their own performance as they could watch it improve over time.

Modelling (answering the question 'what if?') is a difficult concept for students, especially as the examples used are often too difficult for the students to engage with. Making the example tangible (as in the next story) allows the students to visualise the possibilities and discuss the issues (for example why people would want a low fat sandwich). Use of an interactive white board for whole class or small group teaching can similarly engage students with the learning. Allowing students to physically touch the board, and encouraging them to hypothesise and evaluate as changes happen, concurs with the constructivist model of teaching. See **www.mirandanet.ac.uk/ pubs/smartboard.htm**

Classroom story

A Year 8 design and technology project used a failing sandwich company as a focus for a range of problem-solving tasks. The students were faced with the scenario of a sandwich company whose best selling line – cheese sandwiches – were not selling as they should. This was a substantial project, part of which entailed looking at how food products are researched and developed. They weighed the ingredients for their sandwich using accurate electronic scales and then modelled the nutritional analysis of their 'new' sandwich looking at the marketing possibilities (e.g. low fat) and implications for cost of production and the final label. The worksheet below supported the latter part of the activity.

Modelling the nutritional analysis of your sandwich

	Cheddar Cheese	White Bread	Butter	
Weight in grams	24.5	55	10	
Protein per 100g	26	7.8	0.5	Amounts per
Carbohydrate per 100g	0	50	0	100g found in
Kcal per 100g	400	230	750	food tables
Fat per 100g	34	1.7	82	
Protein per weight used	6.37	4.29	0.05	Formulae used
Carbohydrate per weight used	0	27.5	0	to calculate amounts
Kcal per weight used	98	126.5	75	
Fat per weight used	8.33	0.935	8.2	

NUTRITIONAL ANALYSIS OF THE SANDWICH

PROTEIN	10.71	Sum function used
CARBOHYDRATE	27.5	
KCAL	299.5	
FAT	17.465	

Now you are ready to **model** - the example above has been modelled to produce an 'under 300 kcal' sandwich for someone on a calorie-controlled diet. You could try a different one e.g. reduced fat.

Extension - now that you have learned the skill of modelling on a spreadsheet to find the nutritional analysis, see if you can use the same method and sheet to work out the cost of production for your sandwich using the prices below.

Cheese - £5.26 per 1 kg   Butter - £0.57 per 250g   Bread - £0.25 per 250g

Can you suggest a retail price?

There are additional costs (labour, buildings, transport etc.) - £0.25 per sandwich that you must consider. What will your profit be?

All of you will manage to complete the first spreadsheet with formulae and **most** of you will be able to model e.g. an under 300 kcal and a reduced fat sandwich. **Some** of you will have successfully completed the extension task

Figure 2: Worksheet for nutritional analysis of sandwich.

Capacity and range

This feature is concerned with the diversity of ways in which information can be presented, the ability to communicate with people all over the world and the immediacy and availability of information which is up to date, sometimes to the minute and can bring life to research into current issues better than traditional research methods.

Classroom story

A teacher of a Year 9 MFL class found a class of similar age students in France for her students to correspond with using email. The project began very well with the students writing half of their message in the target language and half in their own language. The theme of the first few letters tended to be all about themselves, but subsequent correspondence became difficult for both classes as they were struggling with vocabulary. The teachers realised that they had to work to common themes so that the students' correspondence was an extension activity of the learning taking place in the classroom. Other subject areas became interested to such an extent that it became a cross-curricular project with a focus on festivals and a celebration of cultural diversity. They looked at festivals that were common (such as Christmas and Easter) and those that were unique (for example Guy Fawkes and the French Pepper Festival). Three more schools joined the project from Portugal, Germany and Slovakia.

The following are the types of activity that have subsequently taken place:

- *recording songs in music;*
- *shared assembly on Europe Day – 9 May;*
- *exchanging recipes for use in food technology;*
- *videos of events;*
- *digital images of art work;*
- *a display created in each school, a 'Point Europe', regularly updated with information from all the partners.*

www.gymfilakovo.sk/phare/projects.html
Look at www.epals.com/ to find partners for your students.

The feature of capacity and range can work against a teacher if the lesson isn't well planned. Students can lose valuable time, for example, by scrolling through a clip art gallery rather than doing a focused search or surfing for information from the Internet in an understandable format. One of the features of Microsoft Word is that when the 'enter' key is pressed at the end of a web address it becomes a live link (it changes to blue, is underlined and when the cursor points at it there is the familiar 'pointing hand' denoting a link). Therefore interactive worksheets can be easily produced which students can use 'live' to links which have already been checked for suitability. This is not to say that students should never be offered the opportunity to do a 'free search'. The use of 'key words' and Boolean logic to refine a search on a CD-ROM or in a search engine is an important concept for students to engage with and is relevant to all subject areas. However we would never offer students the entire works of *Encyclopaedia Britannica* or a vast library to search for information without some guidance and it is the same when using computer-based research.

Interactivity

The interactive way in which information can be processed and presented enables teacher and students to explore prepared or constructed models and simulations. They can search for and compare information from other sources, presenting it in a variety of different ways, using a range of technologies thus making it accessible for different audiences. Interactivity actually encompasses many of the other features of ICT, pushing the boundaries of what is possible with the use of technology. The audience and the author are almost indistinguishable as the roles become blurred. Examples can be found particularly in multimedia work and web authoring. The integration of text, graphics, sound, video and hyperlinks allow for the reader to take 'excursions' into the narrative, exploring, researching, exchanging information and learning as they do so.

Visit the Hackney's Hirewire City Learning Centre at **www.highwire.org.uk**

Classroom story

A group of Year 7 students and staff went away for an enrichment week of cross-curricular activities. Each day the students took digital photographs of their experiences and in the evening they word-processed a diary of events. The images and text were then placed on the school website, not only as a record to refer to later but also for family and friends to see what they were up to. The site allowed interaction with those at home by sending messages, which were checked and then read to the whole group in the evenings.

Kettlethorpe High School, Wakefield: www.kettworks.com/

Practical task

Building on the vision of our changing schools, as outlined in Transforming the Way We Learn (DfES 2002), and growth in Internet access from home, school, public libraries and community centres, many activities can now be continued or developed outside of normal school hours. Extend the limitations of your classroom by using a virtual learning environment such as about.think.com/ to extend discussions, exchange ideas, enhance group work, post support material and allow students to submit work. Explore the suggested site for examples of what others in the profession are doing.

The contribution ICT can make to SEN students and inclusion

For further information on supporting SEN students, see Chapter 10.

Various references have already been made about how ICT can be used to support SEN students but as this is such a huge topic it cannot be dealt with adequately in this chapter. Guidance for specific needs can be found at the Becta website, **www.becta.org.uk/**, which provides strategic techniques to help with particular difficulties. There is no doubt however of the contribution that ICT can make to inclusion. Portable writing aids, communication aids and devices, portable computers, screen magnification software, and appropriate keyboard alternatives can help to support inclusive practice.

www.nagcbritain.org.uk/index.html – the National Association for Gifted Children.

www.nasen.org.uk/mainpg.htm – the National Association for Special Educational Needs.

Access

Sufficient access to appropriate and up to date ICT for any student is of course an issue for all students. The *ImpaCT2* report (Becta 2002) reassuringly confirms that connectivity is reaching government targets, with virtually all secondary schools having Internet access. However it also demonstrates a strong relationship between access to the Internet at home and socio-economic status, with those advantaged students spending four times longer using ICT at home compared with at school. An ICT activity doesn't mean that all of the students need to be sitting in a computer suite interacting with a monitor, in fact this is often a sign of poor practice if this is all that occurs. However it does mean that all of the students need to have sufficient time to achieve the learning objectives and this does entail careful planning, keeping abreast of new technologies and not being afraid to have a number of activities happening in the classroom at one time.

Classroom story

A Year 11 GCSE art class visited a sculpture park as part of the research for their coursework. They all wanted to take photographs so that they could manipulate them later on in the computer suite but the teacher was concerned that only one digital camera was available and would mean that not all of the students would have a chance to use it. She decided that all of the students would take conventional photographs using their own cameras (some used disposable ones) and that the images would be put onto photo CD during the processing phase. The images were put onto the school Intranet for all of the students to access in their own time.

Assessment

As part of the Key Stage 3 Strategy, national targets for Key Stage 3 were announced in July 2001. The targets are that:

- **by 2004, 75 per cent of 14-year-olds will achieve level 5 in ICT;**
- **by 2007, 85 per cent will achieve level 5 in ICT.**

This doesn't mean that all teachers are going to be teachers of ICT. The curriculum model of ICT in schools can vary from ICT being taught as a discrete subject to being totally subject-integrated. Whatever your model there will be a member of staff who has responsibility for the co-ordination of ICT within the curriculum as well as assessment. However teachers are often asked to assess students' work for both their own subject area and for ICT. The National Curriculum in Action website at **www.ncaction. org.uk/subjects/ict/index.htm** uses students' work and case study material to show what the National Curriculum in ICT looks like in practice. The examples given show:

- **the standard of students' work at different ages and key stages;**
- **how the programmes of study translate into real activities.**

Practical task

Using students' work from an ICT activity that you have planned, assess the work for your own subject area then look at the work again for its use of ICT. Select what you would consider to be high, middle and low achieving pieces of work and discuss these with the ICT co-ordinator in your school. How did the levels of attainment compare with:

- *the levels in your own subject area;*
- *the Key Stage 3 strategy target levels?*

Were there any other issues that the discussion raised such as suitability of the task, gender bias and access to technology?

ICT for professional purposes

You will notice that a large number of the websites suggested in this chapter include discussion forums for teachers to exchange and share ideas with other professionals. Join one of these forums, read what your new colleagues are doing and be adventurous in your own teaching. Listen to your students, what are they doing with new technologies? Remember that ICT isn't just about working with computers!

Teaching ICT across the curriculum:
a summary of key points

____ *There is no substitute for good teaching. It is crucial that you always question if the planned activity supports the learning objectives for the lesson.*

____ *Never underestimate the ICT capability of students.*

____ *Plan lessons to maximise the use of ICT so that time is not wasted, for example with trouble-shooting equipment, unnecessary searching for sites or formatting without a purpose.*

____ *Develop strategies for linking home, school and the outside world.*

____ *Do not be complacent about your own capability, take advantage of any training that is offered and keep abreast of new technologies.*

Further reading

www.becta.org.uk The British Educational Communications and Technology Agency provides information, advice and dialogue relating to ICT in education, and is an excellent resource for research plus links to other affiliated sites.

www.nc.uk.net/ The government's definitive curriculum site for teachers. It contains not only the National Curriculum but also a wealth of support material especially in support of recent initiatives, plus downloadable files and links.

www.tes.co.uk A monthly insert in the *Times Educational Supplement* called Online contains useful classroom ideas, book reviews and ICT news.

Loveless, A. and Ellis, V. (eds.) (2001) *ICT, Pedagogy and the Curriculum: Subject to Change*. London. RoutledgeFalmer. A provocative collection of essays about the possiblities for ICT in schooling.

For further information on teaching ICT across the curriculum, visit **www.learning matters.co.uk/education/learnteach/chapt8.html**

Glossary

Boolean logic The Internet is a vast computer database and its contents must be searched according to the rules of computer database-searching. Much database-searching is based on the principles of Boolean logic. When using Internet search engines (the most common method of searching), the user is often unaware that this is happening but can be disappointed with the search results. Constructing a logical search using 'or, and, not' (or +, -, = signs) with the search words can refine the search and make the 'hits' much more successful. Visit the following two sites for further information: **www.education-world.com/a_tech/tech001.htm** and **http://computer.howstuffworks.com/boolean.htm**

Capability ICT capability is characterised by an ability to use effectively IT tools and information sources to investigate and research, develop ideas, communicate, analyse and evaluate. It is not concerned with the acquisition of skills but the teaching of these skills may form part of the learning process towards capability. See also Allen (2000, p. 2). *See pages 117–118*

ICT IT is to ICT as literacy is to books, journals or screen displays. The focus of IT is on students' capability with ICT. For this reason IT is the title used for the National Curriculum subject qualifications.

Key skills The six key skill areas which are embedded in the structure of the National Curriculum – communication, application of number, information technology, working with others, improving own learning and performance, and problem-solving.

Logo A programming language plus a philosophy of education developed in the 1960s by Seymour Papert. It was designed as a tool for learning and its features – modularity, extensibility, interactivity, and flexibility follow from this goal. Free Logo software can be found at **www.atlantic.net/-caggiano/logo/index.html** plus research information and additional links.

9 THE 14–19 CURRICULUM

CHRIS MATCHAM

Professional Standards for QTS

 2.1d, 2.3

To be awarded QTS for Key Stage 4 and Post 16, you must be aware of the pathways of progression through the 14-19 phase in school, college and work-based settings. You should be familiar with the Key Skills as specified by QCA and the National Qualifications Framework. You should have knowledge of the progression within and from your own subject and the range of qualifications to which your subject contributes. You must understand how courses can be combined in a student's individual programme.

You should also be aware of the expectations, typical curricula and teaching arrangements in the key stages or phases before and after the ones that you are trained to teach.

Introduction

The 14-19 curriculum is undergoing a period of change designed to bring provision in Key Stage 4 and Key Stage 5 together into a unified framework. This will allow for much greater flexibility in meeting the needs of individual students, whilst meeting the national targets for achievement.

For some time there has been a notion of a coherent 14-19 curriculum. The government-initiated Dearing review of the Post 16 Curriculum (which commenced in the early 1990s and was completed in 1996) took the view that there had to be a much stronger relationship between a student's experience at GCSE and their Post 16 Studies. This led directly to the development of the new structure for A levels introduced in September 2000. However, there are now calls for much more radical and fundamental changes to the 14-19 curriculum. Among these has been *14 and Beyond*, proposals published by the Secondary Heads Association in October 2001. The government itself is committed to the establishment of a 14-19 phase and published a Green Paper, *14–19 Extending Opportunity, Raising Standards* in February 2002. Most recently the Tomlinson Working Group on 14-19 Reform has made radical proposals which, if accepted, would dismantle GCSEs, A levels and vocational qualifications and replace them with a diploma framework. This framework would include a compulsory core in which communication and mathematical skills would play a part. In addition to proposals such as these, for much broader change, there have been a number of smaller developments which have already led to greater coherence for some students and have added to the impetus for broader change.

The need for greater coherence has long existed but has been made more urgent by the government's targets for increasing the number of young people continuing their education beyond 16 and eventually into Higher Education. Dearing also noted in the consultations for his review that the system as it existed then was divisive and far too heavily age-related. The changes to the Post 16 Curriculum that resulted from his review have at least begun to meet these failures although they have been severely hindered by the demands of externally developed assessment structures.

The SHA proposals also promulgated radical change based around the principle of a single framework which provides learning opportunities for all. This has now been echoed by the proposals of the Tomlinson working group. But what frameworks currently exist and how do they support or prevent coherence?

The current situation

Currently a number of different frameworks exist. They can be divided into two categories:

- **those which define the curriculum;**
- **and those which define the organisation of the sector.**

In both cases there have been a number of recent changes which have had significant impact upon the 14-19 sector.

Curriculum frameworks

All qualifications (170,000 in all) have recently been placed into a new National Qualification Framework by QCA. This is intended to make the levels of each qualification and the progression between levels much clearer for all those using the system, as well as ensuring quality. How does the existing curriculum provision for 14-19-year-olds fit into this framework?

KEY STAGE 4

This is the curriculum framework for a student between the ages of 14 and 16. It is currently the law that all students must follow the nationally defined Programmes of Study for English, maths, science, information technology and citizenship. They must also take part in physical education and follow a locally agreed syllabus in religious education. From September 2004 schools must make available to all students who wish to study courses in them a new category called Entitlement Curriculum Areas. These include the arts, design and technology, the humanities and modern foreign languages. Until September 2004 it was possible to disapply some students from areas of the National Curriculum. The changes have meant that this is no longer necessary, although disapplication from science will be allowed until 2006.

Work-related learning also becomes statutory in 2004.

Key Stage 4 qualifications
A number of different qualifications are used by different institutions to accredit achievement at Key Stage 4. They are mainly defined as being at Level 2 (Intermediate Level). They include:

- *GCSE*: Largely academically-based with quite restricted teacher assessment in most subjects. The majority of the assessment is through externally-administered examinations at the end of two years' study. These have recently been reviewed and there have been significant changes in a small number of subjects; for example, the OCR (Bristol Project) geography syllabus where the value of coursework has been increased and examination modules can now be taken earlier in the course and with the opportunity for some re-sitting.

- *V(vocational)GCSE:* These are replacing GNVQ Part I in a range of vocationally-based subjects.
- *Entry Level Qualifications (Level I):* These are offered by some schools to students who are below GCSE level. They can take many different forms, for example as a Certificate of Achievement in a particular subject or as an over-arching certificate made up of individual units such as the National Skills Profile. Currently achievements in these qualifications are not included in the league tables of results.

KEY STAGE 5

At Key Stage 5 there is no prescription of the programme of study or curriculum, other than the requirement for RE and citizenship. A student's programme is developed and agreed through guidance and counselling. It generally reflects their existing qualifications, interests and future career plans. Currently external control of programmes is exercised through the new Post 16 Inspection regime and funding mechanisms.

Key Stage 5 qualifications
- *Intermediate (Level 2):* All of the qualifications taken in Key Stage 4 can also be taken at Key Stage 5. They usually form the core of a programme for students who have not achieved five Cs and above and aspire to do so. Additionally students may take a full GNVQ Intermediate Qualification, which is assessed in a similar way to the Part I but comprises six units. Some students with extended work experience placements may get National Vocational Qualifications (NVQ).

- *Advanced (Level 3):* In September 2000 every aspect of the Post 16 Advanced Curriculum changed. All courses, whether they are academic or vocational are now modular. The different qualifications that could form part of a Post 16 Programme of Study are described below:
  - *AS/A level:* The A level has been divided into two parts. AS is taken in the first year of study. It is assessed in a more straightforward way, which is closer to the style of assessment which the students have already experienced at GCSE. Theoretically it also contains the more straightforward parts of the specification (although this has not always proved to be the case). Students may decide to just take the AS in a subject or continue on to A2 which will give them the full A level. This is assessed in a very complex way and requires more sophisticated understanding.

- *AVCE (Advanced Certificate of Education):* Like the Intermediate Level vocational qualifications, these are related to specific vocational areas. They are taught in units each one of which is assessed by a substantial teacher assessed portfolio and an exam board administered test. They are usually offered as either Single or Double Awards (single being equivalent to an A level , there is no real equivalent to AS).

BTEC qualifications

These qualifications, which have continued to be offered by the FE sector in some vocational areas, are now gaining in popularity in schools as well as colleges. They are offered through EDEXCEL and are mainly taken as Level 2 (BTEC First) and Level 3 (BTEC National) qualifications. Level 1 and Level 4 qualifications are also available.

Key Skills at Key Stage 4 and 5

There is one set of qualifications that operates at all levels of the qualifications framework. These are called Key Skills and are divided into two groups:

Core Key Skills	*Outer Key Skills*
Application of Number	Improving Own Learning and Performance
Communication	Problem Solving
Information Technology	Working With Others

It was intended that they should be delivered across the curriculum. In order to achieve this, opportunities for Key Skills are identified in all of the Advanced, GCSE and Vocational Specifications developed for Curriculum 2000. They are currently mainly taken up in Key Stage 5, although they are beginning to be used at Key Stage 4.

An example of them in operation can be found in the AS Geography Fieldwork Investigation module. This requires the use of statistical techniques (Application of number), report writing skills (Communication), the use of desk-top publishing, data-bases and spreadsheets (IT), devising methods of data collection (Problem-solving), group collection of data (Working with others) and the completion of an action plan (Improving own learning and performance).

Key Skills were given a very high profile in the introduction of Curriculum 2000. Unfortunately, the assessment demands have meant that in practice it has proved very difficult to deliver them across the curriculum. Initially many schools and colleges time-tabled separate lessons for delivering the Core Key Skills in order to meet the demands of the assessment, however many are now drawing back from this position. This is in response to the much publicised assessment overload on the students, and also as result of the lack of recognition by Higher Education of Key Skills qualifications through the UCAS points system.

Some Key Skills are being introduced at Key Stage 4 on an individual basis. For example in some schools Information Technology at Level 2 is being taken by students who have not opted for a GCSE or GNVQ Part One in Information Technology. The Outer Key Skills may well form a part of some of the new Citizenship Qualifications. The Core Key Skills can be assessed as a full certificate at Level 3 (the equivalent of Advanced Level); in practice most institutions are now going for one Key Skill at Level 3 that complements a student's programme of A levels.

Whilst Curriculum 2000 has not been universally well received, largely because of what some teachers see as 'over assessment', it has already had some benefits:

- **the division of A level into two stages has helped students make the step up from GCSE to A level;**
- **the new courses can be used to create much more individual programmes of study which meet students' needs much more accurately;**
- **it is much easier for students to follow a programme which mixes academic and vocational subjects;**
- **the modularity of the courses means that students have some opportunity to retake some of the assessment;**
- **an emphasis on key skills (particularly the outer key skills) can improve a student's independent learning skills.**

The organisational framework

The organisation of 14-19 education varies across the country and is now undergoing major change. Most 14-16 year old students are educated in schools. Since 1998 it has been possible for some students of this age to be educated in Further Education Colleges for part or even all of their courses. Options available Post 16 are entirely dependent on where the student lives, in some areas of the country all Post 16 provision is in Further Education or Sixth Form Colleges, in others they may have a choice between remaining at school or going to college.

From April 2002, all Post 16 provision and Pre 16 vocational provision will be funded by the local Learning and Skills Councils according to a national formula. The Learning and Skills Council will also have some influence over where courses are delivered. At present it is thought that this will mainly be exercised in relation to ensuring access and quality.

Even within schools, timetables are often organised in very different ways at Key Stage 4 and Key Stage 5. For example in some LEAs, all secondary schools and some Further Education Colleges operate to a common half-day blocked timetable to ensure access to as many different choices for students as possible. Schools operate their own separate timetable structure at Key Stage 4.

What have been the problems of implementing change so far?

Up to now the Post 16 curriculum has been subject to most change. The first year of operation of Curriculum 2000 demonstrated that there are clear benefits from the changes as previously identified, but it has also presented many challenges. These have included:

- **Over-timetabling of students. Curriculum 2000 envisaged students completing four/five AS Levels and taking three of these on to A2, along with key skills. In practice it is only the most able who can cope with the demands of such a programme. This has proved particularly difficult for students from less affluent backgrounds who often have to work a substantial number of hours in part-time work in addition to their studies.**

- Over-assessment. Each AS and A2 qualification is composed of three modules, mainly tested by examination. The students could find themselves sitting up to 15 examinations at the end of their first year of study.
- The proliferation of external assessment has led to the examining bodies becoming increasingly unable to cope. This will eventually bring the accuracy of the assessment into question.
- The loss of activities that are not assessed. The increased demands on students' time has meant that a whole range of valuable activities including community placements and support for younger students has been curtailed.
- Students may choose not to continue on to A2 from AS either in all or some of their subjects. This makes planning the provision of viable groups very difficult.

What opportunities already exist for a more coherent 14-19 curriculum?

Although the DfES only published the new National Qualifications Framework in January 2002, there are already some limited opportunities to offer more flexible programmes to students across the 14-19 age range. Some of these are described below:

Work-based learning

All students are expected to receive aspects of work-related learning through their programme of study; for example, in two week work experience placements. However, some are involved in much more focused activity which may involve them in being disapplied from other aspects of their curriculum. This usually applies to students who are disaffected in some way or are unable to access some areas of the National Curriculum. Their work-related learning might involve them in being taken out of part or all of their ordinary timetable to take part in an extended work-experience placement with an employer or a training provider, or alternatively to take a vocational course at a Further Education College.

Technology

Whilst a National Curriculum Programme of Study must be delivered to all students (except those that are disapplied), it does not have to be done in a subject specific way. A number of schools are introducing different ways of delivering technology. For example it could be delivered through art and design, with the opportunity to take an additional product design GCSE. Another alternative would be for all students to take a Vocational GCSE in manufacturing, which is not linked to any specific context, enabling students to have the choice of doing manufacturing in food, textiles, ceramics, resistant materials or even microelectronics.

Changes to assessment regimes

The changes to some of the GCSE specifications have led to much more flexible regimes which have opened new opportunities. For example, in the previously-mentioned OCR GCSE Geography (Bristol Project) syllabus, students are now assessed by three different modules which can be taken at different times during the course. This has opened up the opportunity for students to start their course towards the end of Year 9, complete it in Year 10 and possibly start AS in Year 11. This approach is mirrored in a number of other subjects where the most able students are 'fast tracked', complete their GCSE in Year 10 and do an AS in Year 11. It is one strategy that is being used to extend the most able (often referred to as the Gifted and Talented).

What are the current issues in the 14 -19 curriculum?

It should by now be clear that, at present, whilst there are opportunities to develop both overall coherence and greater flexibility for individual students, the 14-19 curriculum and the organisational framework within which it operates is extremely complex. This presents many challenges for both institutions and students. These include:

- **Ensuring the understanding of the 14-19 curriculum by students and their parents**. Establishing a sophisticated guidance and counselling system to ensure that students make informed choices and then manage their individual timetable. Designing a timetable framework that will enable students to access the greater flexibility.
- **Establishing partnerships between all providers of 14-19 education**. Until recently the system has encouraged competition between providers of 14-19 education. It is clear that if each student is to have their own individual planned programme of study, this may involve them in studying (or training) with more than one provider. In addition to establishing a trusting working relationship, a great deal of time will be needed to provide the support and guidance that the students will need.
- **Improving guidance and counselling**. Students will need a great deal of expert, knowledgeable advice if they are to successfully plot their way through the framework and meet their own individual needs.
- **Establishing the value of 'vocational' qualifications**. Many stakeholders view these as being of lower value than 'academic' qualifications. It will be difficult to develop a more appropriate, flexible curriculum for individual students while this view is still widely held.
- **Ensuring that the provision of high quality learning and teaching is a central objective of any change**. The experience with the introduction of AS/ A2 and Key Skills has tended to be that the demands of the assessment are so great that they have taken time from considering approaches to learning and teaching.

How does this affect students now?

Even in the current situation there are obviously many different programmes of study and routes that individual students could take. In most schools Key Stage 4 options offer students the opportunity to make some choice within a restricted framework.

Described below are three case studies of individual students and possible routes for them in the current environment.

Student A – is academically able and interested. She is predicted to get Level 7 in her Key Stage 3 SATs in the three core subjects. She has no clear focus for her future career, although she is interested in journalism.

- **Key Stage 4 courses – GCSE in maths, double science, English language and literature, geography, media studies, and art and design (including product design), with Key Skill in information technology at Level 2, short courses in RE and French, and timetabled sport.**

- **Key Stage 5 courses – AS in English literature, geography, media studies, psychology and critical thinking. A2 in English literature, geography, media studies. Key Skill in information technology at Level 3.**

Student B – is of average ability. He is predicted to get Level 5 in his Key Stage 3 SATs in the three core subjects, although he may struggle to achieve this in English. He is anxious to get a Modern Apprenticeship with a local Information Communications Technology company at 16.

- **Key Stage 4 Courses – GCSEs in maths, science, English language and literature, resistant materials (technology), microelectronics, VGCSE in information technology with short courses in RE and modern foreign language and timetabled sport.**

- **At 16 he is successful in being accepted for a Modern Apprenticeship. His employer expects him to take Advanced Vocational courses at a local Further Education College as part of his training programme.**

Student C – has learning difficulties that mean that she will find it difficult to achieve above Level 3 in her English SAT at Key Stage 3. In maths and science, where she is allowed to have help with reading in the tests, she is expected to achieve Level 4 or even 5. She finds it difficult to cope in some situations and can behave in a challenging way. She is very interested in a career in caring and has already visited the local home for the elderly.

- **Key Stage 4 – GCSE in English language (with extra support), maths, double science, and art, VGCSE in health and social care (taken at a local FE College), Key Skill in information technology at Level 2, with short course RE , timetabled sport and weekly work experience placement in a local home for the elderly.**

- **At the end of her Key Stage 4 programme she continues somes studies in English, maths, and health and social care in school whilst gaining NVQ qualifications through her placement in a local care home.**

What are the implications for the future?

There has long been a lobby for a coherent 14-19 curriculum. This has been met by a government policy commitment to achieving that coherence. In February 2002 the government published a Green Paper entitled *14-19: Extending Opportunities, Raising*

Standards. The Green Paper is currently in consultation and it is envisaged that proposals that are carried forward will be implemented over a ten-year period. The main proposals contained in the Green Paper are as follows.

- **There should be a matriculation diploma at 19 to be awarded at Intermediate, Advanced or Higher levels. The proposed benchmarks for the three levels give parity of esteem for Vocational and Academic qualifications. This could include an element of work experience. It will be available from September 2007 at the earliest.**
- **The core at Key Stage 4 should comprise English, maths, science and ICT along with citizenship, RE, sex and health education and PE.**
- **A language, an arts subject and a humanities subject must be offered at Key Stage 4 (statutory from September 2004).**
- **A levels to have more demanding questions so that the highest achievers can gain a distinction.**
- **The most able students, as evidenced by their SATs levels at Key Stage 3, may take GCSEs early, or even skip them and go straight to AS levels.**

Many of the proposals, particularly those relating to quality of esteem between the vocational and the academic, were welcomed. There were concerns that there was no move to reduce the examination burden on students and that there was too much emphasis on sub-dividing the elite by putting a distinction into A level with no consideration of those students who might work very hard, but still not be capable of achieving the equivalent of five Cs or above at GCSE.

Many of these proposals have been taken a stage further in the Interim Report of the Working Group on 14-19 Reform chaired by Professor Tomlinson, published in February 2004. The report suggests that all existing qualifications 14-19 be replaced by a unified framework of diplomas, which would be available at four levels: entry, foundation, intermediate and advanced.

All diplomas would comprise a core, a programme of common skills and a main learning programme, which would be chosen by the student.

Practical tasks

Using the subject specifications available on examination board websites compare the subject content and assessment criteria for a GCSE, a VGCSE and Key Skill qualification in Information Technology. You might also compare a GCSE in science with a VGCSE in the same way.

While on placement in a school, investigate the options systems at Key Stage 4 and Key Stage 5. You should investigate what the options are, how they are offered to students, what advice and counselling students receive and how much flexibility, including disapplication, is possible. One way of achieving this would be by structured interviews with a curriculum manager, a pastoral manager and some students.

As consultation on these reforms is ongoing and it is not expected that changes would be fully in place by 2010, a visit to their website is suggested to see how far the consultation has progressed. However, it is likely that some developments in schools and colleges will pre-empt the statutory introduction of the reforms.

The 14–19 curriculum:

a summary of key points

- _____ *The academic/vocational divide continues to exist.*
- _____ *There are attempts to break down the barriers between Key Stage 4 and Key Stage 5.*
- _____ *The effects of Curriculum 2000 at Advanced Level and the implications for the amount of assessment need to be considered.*
- _____ *Opportunities are beginning to develop to enable students to have more individualised programmes that may may be provided from a number of different sources.*
- _____ *There is a clear potential role for Key Skills within the 14–19 Curriculum.*
- _____ *Tomlinson's working group on 14-19 reform propose a complete change in the current system which, if accepted, would lead to huge changes during the next decade.*

Further reading

www.dfes.gov.uk DfES website. Information on the legal requirements, as well as the Programmes of Study for individual subjects.

Examination Board websites. These provide a wealth of information in addition to the specification and assessment information. They often include teacher and student guides, and some have teacher bulletin boards.

Most universities have published documents describing their admissions policy in relation to the new qualifications and key skills framework. You will find that most of these are fairly vague so far.

QCA (2004) *Changes to the Key Stage 4 Curriculum – guidance for implementation from September 2004.*

DfES (2004) *Summary of the Interim Report of the Working Group on 14-19 Reform.* DfES/0219/2004.

For further information on the 14-19 curriculum, visit **www.learningmatters. co.uk/education/learnteach/chapt9.html**

Professional Standards for QTS

→ **1.2, 1.3, 1.6, 3.1.2, 3.1.3, 3.3.3, 3.3.4, 3.3.7, 3.3.9**

To be awarded QTS you must have respect for the differences in learning and development experienced by students and seek to promote the self-esteem of those who find learning difficult. You need to be aware of the variety of ways in which support staff can be used to promote inclusion and must be able to demonstrate the ability to differentiate the curriculum effectively, drawing upon a developmental approach to enabling progression.

You may find it helpful to read through the appropriate section of the handbook that accompanies the Standards for the Award of QTS for clarification and support.

What is inclusion?

The Green Paper (1997) entitled *Excellence for All Children: Meeting Special Educational Needs,* and the DfEE document *Meeting Special Educational Needs: A Programme of Action* (1998) embraced the principle of inclusion and set out in the educational arena the government's aim of social inclusion. The concept of inclusion is more than another word for integration. It embodies Human Rights and Equal Opportunities. Its general principles encompass:

- *Valuing diversity*: all students should be valued. This extends beyond a simplistic view of Special Educational Needs (SEN) and disability. It extends beyond the notion of geographical integration, which is concerned with where **SEN** students are placed.
- *Entitlement*: all students are entitled to receive, with a suitable peer group, a broad, balanced and relevant curriculum.
- *Dignity*: all students, and their parents, are entitled to be treated with respect and have their views taken into account.
- *Individual needs*: inclusive practice should not create situations within which individual needs are left unmet.

An historical overview

Research, policy and practice in the education of students with SEN have moved through three broad stages since the turn of the twentieth century:

- segregation;
- integration;
- inclusion.

In a sense these stages embody philosophical, sociological and political thinking over the years. It is important, therefore, to understand what has gone before in order to grasp the principles of inclusive learning environments and to be sensitive to the underlying issues that inclusion embraces. A closer examination of how the terminology in this field has evolved demonstrates changes in attitude towards those with SEN.

Terms such as handicap, impairment and disability need clarification if we are to understand the evolution of Special Education.

- *Handicap* is defined by the **Oxford English Dictionary** as **'any encumbrance or disability that weighs upon effort and makes success more difficult'.**
- *Impairment* **is a characteristic, feature or attribute within the individual that is long-term and may be the result of disease, injury or congenital conditions.**
- *Disability* **is the loss or limitation of the ability to take part in normal life on an equal level with others. This disability may be 'a physical or mental impairment which has a substantial and long-term adverse effect on his ability to carry out day-to-day activities' (Disability Discrimination Act 1995).**

At the heart of these definitions is the *inability* of the individual who is regarded as presenting problems for society.

Segregation

At the turn of the twentieth century, emphasis was placed upon a student's **handicap** to determine appropriate schooling. The education of students with handicaps was in the hands of the medical profession to a large extent. Categories of handicap and the educational placement of individuals relied upon the medical model of diagnosis and treatment. In the early twentieth century, educational placement was resolved by segregation, according to the individual's handicap. Early special schools were established for those with sensory handicaps, such as deafness and blindness.

The system of categorisation relied heavily upon the concept of defect.

> ... segregated classes and schools that were to be the repositories for all the varied kinds of students that could not fit into the regular class without creating problems for the system ...
>
> Sarason and Doris (1979)

Some of the labels used at that time may appear bewildering and offensive today. Terms such 'deaf and dumb', 'deaf mute' and 'cripple' reflected prevailing attitudes to disability and impairment.

In the late 1970s and the early 1980s the debate raged about the efficacy of special schooling. The predominantly medical model used for the segregation of students was placed under the spotlight. The educational value of special schooling came under fire. At this time, major changes in the curriculum of mainstream schools were occurring, and the introduction of a National Curriculum, with its highly prescribed content, in a sense mitigated against the continuation of special schools. It was suggested that the curriculum in most ESN (Educationally Sub-Normal) special schools was a watered-down version of that provided in mainstream schools. Those who defended the special school system would point to the adaptation of the curriculum to meet the particular needs of the students. There is no doubt that the dedicated staff in these schools possessed specialist qualifications and were often the expert practitioners. However, special education went through a period of turmoil with a ground-swell of feeling that segregation of students needed to be scrutinised in terms of its educational value. New concepts of handicap were emerging which placed less emphasis upon the *individual* defect. More focus was given to the *educational environment*. This paved the way for integration.

Integration

The 1981 Education Act was a landmark in special education and the embodiment of new, radical thinking. The concept of **integration** was embraced and distinguished in three forms.

- **Locational** – a merging of mainstream and special schooling on a single site. This often resulted in special units being attached to mainstream schools.
- **Social** – providing opportunities for 'special' students to participate socially with their 'ordinary' peers. This meant that the 'special' students could share the same social facilities, e.g. use of the playground, dining facilities and out-of-school clubs where appropriate.
- **Functional** – combining features of locational and social integration. This was the fullest form of integration whereby 'joint participation in educational activities'(DES 1978, p. 100-101) was achieved. Students with SEN could join mainstream classes, where appropriate, on either a part-time or full-time basis.

These three forms provided a flexibility of provision that the Warnock Report recommended and took account of a continuum of needs, from severe to mild, which could be catered for by degrees of integration, depending upon the educational needs of the student. This shift in thinking placed educational needs at the heart of solutions. The drive also came from a desire to ensure that all students, regardless of their SEN, should have the opportunity to participate in the wider context that the mainstream school provided and to be 'included' with their peers. Such moves towards integration spawned their own mechanisms for funding, which remain to some extent today. A student with severe learning difficulties could be integrated but would require extra support to do so.

Inclusion

Inclusion embraces aspects of integration but goes beyond this. Inclusive learning and teaching environments will demonstrate flexibility and differentiated learning in order to respond to individual needs. In line with the principles set out in the SEN and Disability Act, (2001, chapter 10) as a teacher, you will be expected to provide suitable learning challenges for *all* students, by planning effectively to overcome potential barriers to learning and by responding to diverse learning needs. In other words, it is about access to the curriculum and to learning for all.

What are Special Educational Needs?

Special Educational Needs is a catch-all term. It is used frequently in schools and often, depending upon who is using the term, it has different significance. However, you must be aware that it is a term that is embedded in current educational thinking and is defined in statutory legislation.

> A child has *special educational needs* if they have a learning difficulty which calls for *special educational provision* to be made for them.
>
> (Education Act 1996, Section 312)

The Education Act gives a clear definition of what can be considered a learning difficulty and what is meant by special provision. This provides us with shared working definitions to ensure that students can be identified and that there is a uniformity of provision nationally for the different categories of needs. The Act makes reference to 'significantly greater difficulty in learning' and the impact of disability on learning. Educational provision for SEN students is regarded as the provision which is *additional* to (or *different* from) that which is offered generally to all students.

All newly qualified teachers should read the *Code of Practice* (DfES 2001) which is available in all schools. This is a guidance document that will inform your practice on issues such as:

- the **Formal Assessment Procedure leading to a Statement of SEN**;
- **characteristics of different categories of SEN**;
- **meeting the needs of different categories of SEN**;
- **monitoring students' progress**;
- **additional resources needed in mainstream schools.**

What are the SEN categories?

The term Special Educational Needs (SEN) has undergone many face-lifts over the years. It may even be feeling somewhat schizophrenic because of the many name-changes it has had over the last 30 years. Nevertheless, the reason why it is constantly under scrutiny is because of its importance in the educational arena. Coping with the range of SEN may seem daunting to a trainee or a newly qualified teacher, and grappling with new terminology – Emotional and Behavioural Difficulties (EBD), ADHD, Dyspraxia, Asperger's Syndrome, to name but a few, may be overwhelming.

Nevertheless, it is important to recognise the various categories of SEN so that you can plan your lessons to ensure that you:

- **set suitable challenges for *all* students**;
- **respond to 'diverse needs'**;
- **provide access to the National Curriculum.**

The Code of Practice exemplifies the following broad categories:

- **Cognition and Learning Difficulties:**
  1. **General Learning Difficulties**
  2. **Specific Learning Difficulties, e.g. Dyslexia, Dyspraxia;**
- **Emotional, Behavioural and Social Difficulties (EBD);**
- **Communication and Interaction Difficulties:**
  1. **Speech and Language Difficulties**
  2. **Autistic Spectrum Disorders, e.g. ADD/ADHD/Asperger's Syndrome;**
- **Sensory and Physical Difficulties:**
  1. **Hearing Impairment**
  2. **Visual Impairment**
  3. **Physical and Medical Difficulties.**

What is 'graduated response' to SEN?

'Graduated response' is a phrase that is used in the Code of Practice and signifies a staged response to the needs of students with SEN. This approach encapsulates the concept of a continuum of needs and is a method of optimising resources available within the classroom and the school to meet differential needs. It is also a way of ensuring that the individual is at the heart of the process. The procedure has been divided into two main parts: School Action and School Action Plus.

School Action

This is the initial stage of support for students. Schools are required to examine their resources to meet the individual needs of a student. Thus, classroom resources are a key feature in the support. Intervention at this level is a question of how the school and its human resources can provide an environment that enables the student to move towards independent learning. Collaboration between subject teachers and the SEN department is conducted to devise the most appropriate, differentiated environment for the student's SEN from within subject and school resources. An Individual Education Plan (IEP) is initiated so that long-term and short-term targets can be monitored carefully to measure progress.

School Action Plus

If a student is making little progress, despite school intervention, and is performing 'substantially below National Curriculum levels expected for students of a similar age' (DfEE 1999), schools may need to consider seeking advice from outside agencies, such as support services provided by the LEA and other agencies. For example, a school may consult the psychological services to conduct a detailed, specialist assessment of the student's needs to inform further planning and to consider a range of different teaching approaches.

The subject teacher's role

As part of your professional duties you will be monitoring the progress of students in your care. As the person at the coalface, so to speak, you will have opportunities to observe how students learn and to monitor and record their level of achievement in your classroom. You are, therefore, in an ideal position to identify individual strengths and weaknesses. It is your responsibility to initiate the School Action stage of identification of needs. Your concerns about a student who does not appear to be achieving as you would expect will be discussed with your head of department or the school's SENCO (SEN Co-ordinator). At this stage, it is important to record and to gather evidence of the student's progress.

Gathering evidence

This will be done as part of your normal duties and will consist of some, if not most, of the following:

- **observation of the student's response to interactive oral work;**
- **class/group files for comparative purposes;**
- **mark book records;**
- **National Curriculum levels;**
- **attainment levels within the National Literacy Framework;**
- **samples of the student's work output.**

You may also want to look at school records for standardised assessment in reading, spelling and non-verbal reasoning.

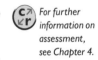 *For further information on assessment, see Chapter 4.*

If you are concerned that a student's behaviour is a barrier to learning, it is important to keep records of:

- **the *type* of behaviour which is cause for concern, for example, anti-social behaviour directed at peers in the form of defiling others' work; or verbally abusive responses to peers and/or the teacher;**
- **the *frequency* of the behaviour;**
- **when the behaviour occurs – to examine patterns of behaviour and triggers. For example, a student may demonstrate disruptive behaviour when working in groups. The behaviour may occur on specific days in which case it may be necessary to look at his/her timetable to find out if there is any significance to the occurrence;**
- **the degree of severity – this can be subjective but will always be made in the context of the school's rules concerning acceptable behaviour.**

What is an IEP?

An Individual Education Plan (IEP) is a working document which is shared by the teacher, the student and the parent. It sets outs to record the provision 'which is additional to, and different from, the differentiated curriculum' for all children in the school (DfEE 10/99).

A good IEP should adhere to the following guidelines:

- **clearly written with measurable targets wherever possible;**
- **three or four focused, short-term targets;**
- **appropriate teaching strategies;**
- **additional provision, e.g. the use of a lap-top in specified lessons; or the additional support of an LSA (Learning Support Assistant) in specified lessons;**
- **criteria for success so that the student, the parent and teacher can measure when a target has been achieved;**
- **review procedures clearly stated.**

What is a Statement of Special Educational Needs?

You will come across 'Statemented' students in your class. This means that these students have a Statement of their Special Educational Needs. A Statement is given to students with severe and complex difficulties that cannot be met within the school's resources. This Statement is a legally binding document issued by the LEA after a consultative process with the school, parents and outside agencies. The Statement specifies the student's SEN and sets out the type of provision needed to meet the individual's needs. This Statement must be reviewed annually.

As a newly qualified teacher you will be given guidance from the special needs department on the best ways to meet the student's needs in your classroom.

Inclusive teaching and learning environments

Creating an inclusive learning environment in your classroom will ensure that all students, regardless of their SEN, can make the most of their potential and can experience success in their learning. Inclusive environments will ensure that the barriers to learning are minimised.

> Pupils with SEN should have the same opportunities as others to progress and demonstrate achievement.
>
> (DfEE 1997, 1:24)

This means that you will be expected to differentiate your teaching. Differentiation is about ensuring that the way you teach and what you teach matches the individual student's needs. *How* you teach will take account of differentiated learning.

> If a child cannot learn the way you teach, you must teach the way s/he learns.
> (Chasty 1990 p. 269, cited in Pumfrey and Elliott 1990)

Considering the variety of SEN categories, mentioned previously in this chapter, which you could encounter in your classroom, planning differentiated work and providing differentiated delivery may appear to be daunting, if not overwhelming, for the NQT. It is vital, therefore, that some general principles are adhered to so that you can develop good practice which can then be modified to meet the more complex needs of some students.

General teaching strategies for SEN

Responding to students' diverse needs and overcoming potential barriers to learning will help to ensure that you provide equality of opportunity for learning. You should bear in mind the following when planning your lessons for students with SEN.

- **A multisensory environment**: this means that you need to give careful consideration to the fact that students learn in different ways. Some are visual learners; some auditory learners and some learn by doing (kinaesthetic learners). Thus, the way in which you present information to your students and the way you expect them to interact with the information and knowledge should tap into as many of these senses as possible.
- **Staged support**: in planning your lessons you must work out different levels of knowledge and understanding for a topic. You must consider what a student should know, and what a student must know within curriculum topics. In other words you will be differentiating basic knowledge from more in-depth knowledge. By asking yourself these fundamental questions you will be able to work out how you can develop competence and skills to match the student's SEN.
- **Provide structure**: this means that you will devise tasks for classroom activities and for assessment purposes whereby you have broken down the process of learning to provide practical, step-by-step procedures while the student is gaining confidence and skills.
- **Provide success**: this may seem obvious and a goal to which all teachers aspire. You must remember that success is very individual but essential for building up self-confidence as a learner. This is especially the case with secondary school students with SEN who may have experienced failure in the past and as a result have become de-motivated or anxious about new learning situations. If you examine what the student can do, you can use her/his knowledge and skill as a springboard so that s/he feels secure in the initial stages of learning a new concept and then gradually moves to new challenges. Providing success is more than the metaphorical pat on the back. Secondary school students with SEN are sensitive to praise and can often see through the empty 'well done' phrase dished out too often. If praise is to be effective and credible, you must let the students know what they have done that is successful. Thus, **targeted praise** is essential. For example, 'good work' is vague and does not let the student know what s/he has done which was good. You must target a skill which the student has used so that s/he learns to use skills and knowledge effectively. In this way you will help students to become aware of their own learning (metacognition), and you will help them to generalise skills to new learning situations. Targeted praise would then become: 'This lab report is well presented in a scientific way.' Thus, you have spelled out for the student that the way s/he has written is appropriate for the type of task.
- **Model the skills**: if you expect your students to be able to take and make notes by the end of Stage 4, demonstrate a variety of ways of presenting information as you are introducing new concepts and information. However, if this is to be effective it is vital that you make your modelling explicit and point out to the students that you have demonstrated the different ways of writing down information. In this way you can model how to use flow charts, bullet points etc.

- **Effective management of LSAs**: remember that LSAs should be used to help develop a student's independence, not to create a dependency culture. Ask yourself the question: what do I want these students to do as a result of this lesson/series of lessons (learning outcomes)? A long-term target for a student may be that you want him/her to be able to read your worksheets in class. In the short-term, getting an LSA to read for the student may seem the best solution. This may well get over the decoding difficulties which the student is experiencing. You might consider using the LSAs' time more creatively by getting them to record frequently used worksheets on audio tape so that the student can be more independent and still has access to your texts while developing decoding skills. This is a scaffolded approach to teaching and learning (Vygotsky 1962). Directing LSA time to the re-presentation of frequently used texts (see guideline further in the chapter) may provide differentiated worksheets which are more accessible for students with SEN.

Manageable solutions

What do students find difficult to cope with in lessons?

You can greatly improve the quality of the learning experience in your classroom and ensure that you consider student diversity by examining the main components of lessons with which SEN students in general have difficulty.

POTENTIAL STICKING POINTS IN LESSONS FOR SEN STUDENTS
- **Verbal instructions.**
- **Written instructions.**
- **Reading.**
- **Writing.**

Verbal instructions

- Think about **when** you are going to give the instructions. SEN students often tire easily in lessons – students are often at their most receptive at the beginning of your lesson. Do not leave giving out vital homework instructions to the end of the lesson as the bell is sounding. This will distract those with ADD/ADHD, for example, and they will not even 'hear' your vital instructions.
- Try to stagger the amount of information you give – setting up the lesson with all the instructions at once is placing extra pressure upon those with specific short-term memory difficulties, for example.
- Provide alternative formats – some students do not take in information if it is only given verbally and may need the backup of a flow chart of simple instructions. (This is multisensory and differentiated learning.)
- Allow some students to tape record verbal instructions which they can play back when memory goes into overload and so that you help them with language processing. This will enable them to hear the instructions again and again without constantly asking you to repeat – less frustrating for them, for you and for the rest of the group!

Written instructions

- Beware of one channel of taking in information, for example the auditory channel is one way of taking in information by listening. If all-important instructions are only given in written form this makes it more difficult for the auditory learner. It will also create difficulties for those whose reading skills are hesitant or weak.
- Provide alternative formats – some students do not take in information if it is only given in written format and may need the back-up a flow chart of simple instructions. (This is multisensory and differentiated learning.)
- Do not put vital instructions only on the board. Often SEN students are not quick enough to take down these instructions and miss out what you want them to do. Provide some typed instruction cards to distribute amongst groups. In this way you will not single out SEN students who may be sensitive to having 'different' work from their peers.
- Keep the instructions clear and *simple*. Often NQTs try to give too many instructions and make the instructions unnecessarily complicated, thinking they are helping SEN students by expanding upon the information. Clear, boxed information with practical sub-headings will direct the student and help those with language processing difficulties to make sense of written instructions.

Example:

What you have to do
Write THREE note points about …

How to make a start
Use your classroom handouts to highlight relevant information.
Use the textbook to find out more information.
List all your information.
Decide upon the best order to present your notes.

Worksheet production

Secondary school students have grown up in a world of computer graphics and sophisticated animation. Often teachers try to emulate these features and try to produce entertaining worksheets. This may be admirable but, if such worksheets are simply provided for visual impact, they may sadly miss the target for SEN students who experience difficulties and worries about accessing texts and worksheets. Worksheets which are too fussy and contain too many graphics and unrelated pictures are confusing for a student who is trying to make sense of the written word. These students will use pictures and graphics to help them to unravel the text so you must ensure that anything you use is complementary and is an alternative, visual method of presenting the written text or prose, not something which you have zapped in from a clipart program because it brightens up the worksheet!

GUIDELINES FOR WRITING WORKSHEETS

- Use of *Comic Sans* font is easier on the eye for those with reading difficulties.
- Key vocabulary in **bold** text.
- Use of colour – key words, for example, could always be in red. This ensures that these words stand out and those with hesitant reading skills can be taught to skim more effectively.
- Layout of written text – uncluttered information is easier to access for those with literacy difficulties. If you put boxes around information you will help the students to 'see' that certain information is linked and goes together.
- Visual representations in tandem with prose.
- Talking worksheets – these are ways of providing a multisensory environment. Your worksheets can be accessed by the 'read back' facilities of a number of computer programs.

Practical task

Design a worksheet for use with a class that contains students with reading difficulties. Incorporate at least three of the above features. Trial this with your class and find out which features of your design provided the best help.

Writing

Modelling how to go about the writing *process* for your subject is important for SEN students. You will provide them with glimpses of 'how the expert goes about the task', and will ensure that you are tapping into different learning styles. Showing students examples of the finished product, e.g. a lab report, may help students to 'see' the way the written work is presented but does not help students to understand the process involved in writing for different subject purposes.

Guided practice is essential for all students but the way in which you manage this for SEN students is critical. You must embody the principles of inclusive learning environments. Thus, you must ensure that you provide structured practice to meet the individual's needs and his/her stage of learning. It is important to provide opportunities which start at the point of need and extend the student's learning.

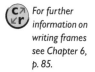 *For further information on writing frames see Chapter 6, p. 85.* Writing frames are an excellent example of this. You can provide as much or as little as is needed to get the student started with writing. Key words, phrases or starting sentences are graduated ways of developing writing. Report writing for scientific purposes, giving an account of a field trip in geography etc. all lend themselves to writing frames.

A word of warning is needed, however. Remember that writing frames are a means to an end and should not be regarded as the pinnacle of achievement for those who are experiencing writing difficulties. Rather they should be considered as a stepping stone – or scaffold – to success.

Managing students with emotional and behavioural difficulties (EBD)

Students who find it difficult to concentrate for periods of time, who cannot seem to sit still in the classroom, who are verbally or physically abusive to their peers and/or their teachers or whose behaviour is considered anti-social, soak up a considerable amount of a teacher's time and energy. It is vital that instructions, both verbal and written, and tasks are carefully planned and designed so that learning is in small steps. Ensure that academic tasks are broken down so that attention span is constantly stimulated.

For further information see Chapter 5, Managing Behaviour for Learning.

Managing the working environment for these students is essential so that opportunities for poor and unacceptable behaviour are minimised. By adopting the solutions in the previous section, you will begin to provide a more secure learning environment for EBD students.

In addition to these generic solutions, consideration should be given to the following:

- **Make explicit your classroom ground rules**. You must demonstrate some flexibility in what you expect these students to achieve whilst not compromising your authority with the class as a whole. One of the most effective ways of doing this is to draw up a learning and behaviour contract with the student and discuss this with him/her. This individual approach will give you a chance to show the student that you are prepared to be firm but fair in dealing with his/her particular situation but that there are lines which you will not expect the student to cross. However, remember that teenagers do not show any appreciation for your considerations!
- **Be consistent**. You must always deal with disruptive behaviour consistently. This provides the EBD student with a sense of security and reinforces the rules for classroom behaviour. It strengthens your discipline by demonstrating fairness – an attribute highly regarded by all children!
- **Keep calm and try to avoid losing your temper**. This seems such an obvious statement but one which has to be worked on when dealing with difficult classroom behaviour. Some students seem to take pleasure from trying to get their teachers angry. Remember they are past masters at argument, shouting out and causing disruption. Counter this behaviour with even, quiet speech and measured actions. Try not to retaliate when these students shout abusively but rather mentally count to ten and go over to their working area so that you minimise the upheaval. This type of restraint which is non-invasive can be most effective not only with the specific student but also your standing with the class in general.
- **Give consideration to the specific praise and rewards for individual students**. These will be effective if the EBD student really perceives the rewards as something which is valued in the culture. What you might regard as a reward may be of no value to the teenager. Discussing rewards with the individual can ensure greater success.

Inclusion: Special Educational Needs:
a summary of key points

___ *Read the Code of Practice for SEN to familiarise yourself with the different categories of learning needs and some general guidance for teaching.*

___ *Examine your lesson planning to incorporate both a variety of modes of delivery of information and a range of activities to meet differing learning styles and abilities.*

___ *Ensure that you weave in the principles of good practice to provide a differentiated curriculum that enables students to participate in the academic tasks you set, mindful of realistic targets for individual students.*

___ *Inclusive learning environments will be multisensory, provide structure and, where necessary, give opportunities for 'small step' learning (staged support).*

___ *Make opportunities for modelling and guiding the learning process.*

Further reading

Cheminais, R. (2000) *Special Educational Needs for Newly Qualified and Student Teachers.* London. David Fulton. This is a practical, easy-to-read guide for newly qualified teachers. It provides brief descriptions of the various categories of Special Educational Needs and there is a section on planning for progression.

Qualifications and Curriculum Authority (1998) *Supporting and Target Setting Process: Guidance for Effective Target Setting for Pupils with Special Educational Needs.* London. DfEE/QCA. This document is also practical and gives a wealth of information about how to tackle the teaching of those with different Special Educational Needs.

Stakes, R. and Hornby, G. (2000) (2nd ed.) *Meeting Special Needs in Mainstream Schools: A Practical Guide for Teachers.* London. David Fulton. This is an accessible guide for busy, newly qualified teachers. It provides information to help you develop strategies for classroom management.

For further information on inclusion: special educational needs, visit **www.learning matters.co.uk/education/learnteach/chapt10.html**

Glossary

Attention Deficit Disorder (ADD) or Attention Deficit Hyperactivity Disorder (ADHD). Students who have been diagnosed with these disorders are recognisable in class because they can only concentrate for very short periods and often fidget and move around the class. They are often distracted by 'working' noise in the classroom and may behave inappropriately.

Asperger's Syndrome is a form of autism. Many students who are identified are at the higher academic level of the autistic spectrum. They are often characterised by their difficult or unusual behaviour and their lack of social skills may cause problems in the classroom.

Auditory Learners Some students may identify themselves as 'auditory learners'. These are students who believe they remember information more effectively if they listen to the teacher or work in groups where they can listen to verbal accounts.

Autistic Spectrum Disorders There are many disorders which are associated with autism. The degree of severity is the way in which many are distinguished. ADD, ADHD and Asperger's Syndrome all form part of this continuum. Other associated disorders are speech, language and non-verbal communication disorders. Students who fall within this continuum have varying degrees of difficulty in social interaction.

Dyslexia/Specific Learning Difficulties Dyslexia is best described as a combination of abilities and difficulties which affect the ability to process symbolic information in either alphabetic, numeric or musical notation. Acquisition of literacy and basic numeracy is also affected. Most dyslexic students have weaknesses with working memory, sequencing and organisation. Some may be creative and demonstrate a discrepancy between oral and written performance in class.

Dyspraxia Dyspraxic students often appear clumsy and have difficulty in planning and carrying out complex movements. This sometimes affects their handwriting and motor control. They often take much longer than their peers to produce written work in class. Some dyspraxic students have difficulties co-ordinating the muscles needed for speech production.

EBD Emotional and Behavioural Difficulties.

Kinaesthetic Learners Some students may identify themselves as 'kinaesthetic learners'. These students believe they like to learn 'by doing'. They learn best by experiential learning.

General Learning Difficulties Students with general learning difficulties will experience all-round difficulties in conceptualising and have been labelled as 'moderate or mild learning difficulties' or 'slow learners'.

Hearing Impairment Students with a hearing impairment may experience some degree of hearing loss. Some students may have a severity of loss and require extra resources to access the curriculum. In severe cases the teacher will be expected to wear a radio microphone to enable the student to access verbal information.

Meares-Irlen/Scotopic Sensitivity Syndrome This is a perceptual problem caused by light sensitivity. Students identified with this difficulty will have experienced difficulties with reading. Problems appear to be worse with black print on a white background. This has implications for the use of black markers on white boards. Often the mild difficulties can be remedied by the use of an appropriate coloured overlay on text and photocopied handouts on coloured paper to suit individual needs. Some students may have tinted/coloured lenses with spectacles. The colour of the spectacles' lenses and the overlays are not usually the same colour. Spectacles are useful for reading from a white board or overhead projector transparency.

Visual Impairment Students with a visual impairment may experience some degree of sight loss. Some students may have a severity of loss and require extra resources to access the curriculum, such as brailled text or special software for computers to enable the student to use a word processor.

11 EQUALITY AND INCLUSION
JOHN CLAY AND ROSALYN GEORGE

Professional Standards for QTS

 1.1, 1.2, 1.3, .1.4, 1.5, 1.6, 1.8, 2.4

To be awarded QTS you must have high expectations of all students and respect their social, cultural, linguistic, religious and ethnic backgrounds. Along with this, you should be committed to raising the educational achievement of all students. You should also be aware of, and work within the statutory frameworks relating to teachers' responsibilities. A deep understanding and commitment to these values is a pre-requisite for the effective implementation of the following Standards.

You should treat pupils consistently, with respect and consideration, and be concerned for their development as learners. You are expected to demonstrate and promote the positive values, attitudes and behaviour that you expect from your students. You should communicate sensitively and effectively with parents and carers, recognising their roles in pupils' learning, and their rights, responsibilities and interests. You should be committed to taking part in the corporate life of the school, and understand the contribution that support staff and other professionals make to teaching and learning. You should be able to improve your own teaching, by evaluating it, learning from the effective practice of others and from evidence. You should take increasing responsibility for your own professional development.

You may find it helpful to read through the appropriate section of the handbook that accompanies the Standards for the Award of QTS for clarification and support.

Introduction

Changing contexts: driving up standards

There have been significant changes in the educational climate over the past five years. The election of New Labour in 1997 heralded a range of new initiatives under the heading of modernisation. The White Paper *Excellence in Schools* (DfEE 1997) emphasised the need for education to offer 'equality of opportunity and high standards for all' (p. 3). This has meant in practice, a renewed emphasis on literacy and numeracy and the setting of ambitious targets to raise attainment. The testing at 7, 11 and 14 that now underpins the primary and Key Stage 3 Strategies allows the system to monitor the outcomes at these different stages of schooling and this has been the mechanism used to 'drive up' standards. However, such an approach, which recognises and privileges the view that differences in attainment alone prevents individuals and groups from participating fully in the social, political and economic spheres, is highly problematic and contentious. Nevertheless, the focus on raising standards and promoting inclusion through education will therefore inform this chapter. As a consequence, equality of opportunity has been incorporated and subsumed within the wider agenda of inclusion.

Issues of equality and inclusion underpin the very foundations of the kind of society that we live in; how we relate to each other at the local, national and international level. Within this wider context, it is broadly accepted that education and schooling has a pivotal role in preparing future citizens to embrace the richness and potentialities of diversity and difference. Through an examination of the three central inequalities in education, namely, gender, 'race' and social class, we will explore:

- **what inclusion and equality means in schooling and education;**
- **the legislative framework;**
- **the differential patterns of achievement and expectations of pupils and students from within different communities, schooling and educational systems.**

Equality

In the context of education and schools, the terms equality, equal opportunity and equality of opportunity are used interchangeably as though they all mean the same. This is not the case and Hill and Cole (1999) succinctly sum up the differences. They maintain that:

> a distinction needs to be made between equal opportunities on the one hand, and equality on the other. Equal opportunities policies, in schools and elsewhere, seek to enhance social mobility within structures, which are essentially unequal. In other words, they seek a meritocracy, where people rise (or fall) on merit, but to grossly unequal levels or strata in society — unequal in terms of income, wealth, life-style, life-chances and power. Egalitarian policies, policies to promote equality, on the other hand, seek to go further. First, egalitarians attempt to develop a systematic critique of structural inequalities, both in society at large and at the level of the individual school. Second, egalitarians are committed to a transformed economy, and a more socially just society, where wealth and ownership is shared far more equally, and where citizens (whether young citizens or teachers in schools, economic citizens in the workplace or political citizens in the polity) exercise democratic controls over their lives and over the structures of the societies of which they are part and to which they contribute. While equal opportunities policies in schools and elsewhere are clearly essential, egalitarians believe that they need to be advocated within a framework of a longer-term commitment to equality. Where they are not, the false assumption has been made that there is a 'level playing field', on which we all compete as equals.
>
> (Hill and Cole 1999, pp. 111-112)

Richardson and Wood (1999) argue that within the context of education:

> *equal opportunities* is concerned with ensuring that all pupils and students have genuine access to the curriculum, and that none are at an unfair disadvantage, because their distinctive experiences, concerns and identities are disregarded. The wider political task is to create and enforce legislation against unfair discrimination, both direct and indirect, in all major areas of social life, particularly in employment.
>
> (Richardson and Wood 1999, p. 15)

Some of the ideas embedded in these statements are complex, but despite this complexity, can be translated into everyday issues and contexts that are relevant and meaningful to teachers and learners and will enable them to develop a deeper insight into the way our society is organised, how it operates and how this in turn impacts on schools and other educational establishments.

Practical task

Discuss with another trainee teacher the following key statements, which are intended to provoke debate and discussion.

- *The classroom can be seen as a microcosm of society.*
- *The education system and the school reflect and reproduce society's values.*
- *Knowledge selected for use in schools represents a particular view of the society, the perceived needs of individual, and the intrinsic value and logic of the knowledge itself.*
- *Behaviour that leads to the discrimination of others is learned and sometimes taught by commission and omission.*
- *Challenging inequalities (and supporting young people to do the same) is the responsibility of the teacher through the formal, informal and hidden aspects of the school.*
- *All subject areas and teachers can play a part in tackling inequality and discrimination.*

Inclusion

Like equality and equal opportunities the term inclusion has also become a 'catch all' phrase. The term **social inclusion** refers to participation in society. It includes involvement in politics, the economy and mainstream cultural life. Its opposite is 'social exclusion', for example, the absence of black and other minority people from key areas of social, political, recreational and economic life. Education in relation to social inclusion is concerned with equipping people with knowledge and skills, and also the paper qualifications ('educational achievement'), which they need for full participation in society. The wider political task is to combat poverty, inequality, unemployment, poor housing and poor health (Richardson and Wood, op.cit. p. 15). Social deprivation that arises out of poverty, inequality, unemployment, poor housing and poor health is measured crudely within the schooling system in terms of students' entitlement to 'free school meals'.

What is an Inclusive School?

An inclusive school is one in which the teaching and learning, achievements, attitudes and wellbeing of every young person matter. Effective schools are educationally inclusive schools. This shows not only in their performance, but also in their ethos and their willingness to offer new opportunities to students who may have experienced previous difficulties. This does not mean treating all students in the same way. Rather it involves taking account of students' varied life experiences and needs.

In *Evaluating Educational Inclusion: Guidance for Inspectors and Schools* (Ofsted 2000), it seems that the most effective schools are ones that do not take educational inclusion for granted. Instead, they constantly monitor and evaluate the progress each student makes, identifying students who may be missing out, difficult to engage, or feeling some way apart from what the school seeks to provide. They take practical steps – in the classroom and beyond – to meet students' needs effectively and promote tolerance and understanding in a diverse society (p.4).

During the past three to four years, the term inclusion has gained sufficient currency to become a central feature of the revised National Curriculum and a focus of the Ofsted inspection framework. The National Curriculum Inclusion Statement requires schools, in planning and teaching the curriculum, to take regard of the following three essential principles:

- **setting suitable learning challenges;**
- **responding to the diverse needs students bring to their learning;**
- **overcoming potential barriers to learning and assessment for individuals and groups.**

(Each of the above three principles have been expanded and exemplified in the National Curriculum handbook with additional information on inclusion included in the subject booklets.)

Making your school more inclusive

- **There needs to be a strong commitment to equal opportunities and social justice underpinned by explicit support from the head teacher.**
- **The perspectives of both student and parents needs to be sought.**
- **Clear procedures for recording and acting on racist/sexist incidents must be developed.**
- **An ethos that is open and vigilant, which enables students to discuss issues of justice and equity and shared concerns, needs to be generated and sustained.**
- **Communicating high expectations accompanied by a clear view that under-performance by any group is unacceptable.**
- **Reviewing curricular and pastoral approaches to ensure their sensitivity and appropriateness.**
- **Using ethnic monitoring and other forms of data collection as a routine and rigorous part of the school's/LEA's self-evaluation and management.**

The legal framework

All teachers need to be aware of the legislation with regard to equal opportunities since this has a direct impact on the school's role as a provider and an employer. The legislation is fairly complex in relation to gender, 'race' and Special Educational Needs. It is important to note that since the passing of the 1988 Education Reform Act (ERA) governing bodies have increased responsibility for all aspects of staffing, training and grievance procedures. The specific laws that have been passed in this field are:

- **The Sex Discrimination Act 1975;**
- **The Race Relations Act 1976 (as amended by the Race Relations Amendment Act 2000);**
- **The Education Act 1981 – provision for children with Special Educational Needs;**
- **The Disability Discrimination Act 1995;**
- **Crime and Disorder Act 1998;**
- **Special Educational Needs Code of Practice 2001;**
- **The Employment Equality (Sexual Orientation) Regulation 2003.**

From 1988 to 2003, the Local Government Act (1988), Section 28, made it unlawful for local education authorities to 'promote homosexuality as a pretended family relationship'. You may have heard about Section 28 – but it was repealed in September 2003. Ellis (2004) has shown that young people who identify as lesbian, gay or bisexual still experience problems related to their sexual identity in school, even though sexuality is talked about more in lessons. The Employment Equality (Sexual Orientation) Regulations that became law in December 2003 protect lesbian, gay and bisexual people (including teachers) at work – direct discrimination, indirect discrimination and harrassment are all included in the legislation.

The Race Relations Act 1976 (as amended by the Race Relations [Amendment] Act 2000) places a new general (statutory) duty on public authorities (including schools) to promote race equality. The general duty has three parts:

- **eliminating unlawful race discrimination;**
- **promoting equality of opportunity;**
- **promoting good relations between people from different racial groups.**

Specific duties (also statutory) are laid down in the Act to assist schools in meeting the general duty and include:

- **a proactive approach, which builds race equality into the mainstream of schools and their existing mechanisms;**
- **a requirement for schools to prepare and maintain a written Race Equality Policy;**
- **this policy must deal with race equality explicitly and transparently;**
- **promote race equality and tackle discrimination.**

This policy must also link with other policies and its impact on staff, students and parents from different racial groups must be monitored and evaluated, with particular attention being paid to student attainment.

In practice this means:

- **collecting, comparing and evaluating data to measure performance and effectiveness;**
- **monitoring attainment and progress, exclusions, support and guidance, parental involvement, governing body membership, punishments and rewards;**
- **evaluating data, establishing what more should be done, revising and setting targets in strategic plans.**

Further guidance on the Race Relations Act 1976 (as amended by the Race Relations [Amendment] Act 2000) can be obtained from the Commission for Racial Equality at **www.cre.gov.uk**

Assessing and monitoring the impact of policies

Questions for assessing the impact of a school's policies, including its race equality policy, could include the following:

- **Does the school help all its students to achieve as much as they can, and get the most from what is on offer, based on their individual needs?**
- **Which groups of students are not achieving as much as they can? Why not?**
- **Is the school making sure that its policies, including its race equality policy, are not having an adverse impact on students, parents or staff from racial groups?**
- **How does the school explain any differences? Are the explanations justified? Can they be justified on non-racial grounds, such as English language difficulties?**
- **Does each relevant policy include aims to deal with differences in students' attainments (or possible differences) between racial groups? Do the policy's aims lead to action to deal with differences that have been identified (for example extra coaching for students or steps to prevent racist bullying)?**
- **What is the school doing to raise standards, and promote equality of opportunity for students who seem to be underachieving and who may need extra support?**
- **What is the school doing to:**
  - **prepare students for living in a multi-ethnic society?**
  - **promote race equality and harmony?**
  - **prevent or deal with racism?**

Dealing with racial and sexual harassment

Whilst harassment may be difficult to define it encompasses unwelcome physical, verbal or non-verbal conduct, which may be degrading, abusive and/or offensive. A resolution carried by the European Commission's Council of Ministers (May 1990) suggests that the aim of employer policies should be 'to create a climate at work in which men and women respect one another's human integrity'. We have to acknowledge that harassment is frequently a function of power where power is exercised indiscriminately to the detriment of human rights. Research has indicated that harassment in schools of both a sexual and racial nature or of a more general form is a common part of a student's everyday experience. Often sexual or racial harassment in schools is not regarded as a problem because there have been few complaints. The reason for this may be that recipients:

- **believe no action will be taken;**
- **are too embarrassed to make a complaint;**
- **fear reprisals for making a complaint.**

Classroom story

To whom this may concern.

The girls in this class have put together their feelings towards the boys also in this class. Eversince we went into this class there has been nothing but harrisment. By now we are pretty sick of it all. if nothing is done about it we shall be forced to play truant. The facts are when we are sitting in the class we are violently assaulted, if we do not agree with them they threaten us and hit us if we answer them back. Sometimes when we want to show our feelings to them, they give us agravation. These is also a problem with them calling us insulting names, such as slags, bitch tramps, smelly cows fish, ugly wretch, and lots of other discusting names. Followed by a punch. They don't always hit us, unless we have sweet's or something that they want. We all must state that it is not all off the boys in this class but a vast magority of them. if one of the boys start then normally the rest follow. We must confess that it is also effecting our work and giving is great stress and worry. There are so many problems that we cant take anymore

I hope there is something you can do to help us in the future. Thankyov.

Figure I: Letter from a group of girls.

Practical task

Read the letter 'To whom it may concern'. What action do you think should be taken in the light of this letter, which the headteacher has just received? What should be in place to prevent a situation like this occurring?

(Schools are required to have a behaviour policy under Circular 10/99 that may include provision on dealing with bullying and harassment or a separate policy on harassment that is cross-referenced to the behaviour policy. The policy or policies should include clear procedures on dealing with such incidents.)

Including everyone in educational success

Closing the gap in educational attainment between various groups in society has been widely acknowledged as a pressing concern of national importance. However, it needs to be acknowledged that each of the main ethnic groups now achieve higher attainments than ever before. However since the introduction of the GCSE there has been increasing concern amongst politicians, policy makers, parents etc that has focused upon the differences in achievement between boys and girls.

Gender is also only one factor that affects schooling and achievement. Other factors such as class and ethnicity are strong determinants of educational achievement and thus it is dangerous and inaccurate to imply that all boys underperform and all girls do well. The gender gap is widest in comprehensive schools and least pronounced in independent and grammar schools.

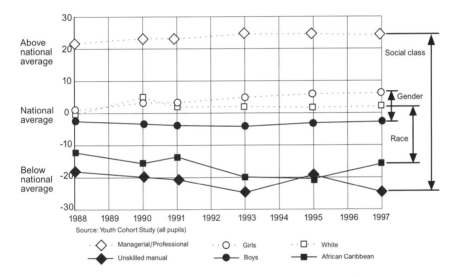

Figure 2: Attainment inequalities by 'race', class and gender, England and Wales, 1988-1997 (five or more higher grade GCSEs relative to the national average).

Figure 2 illustrates how the gender gap is significantly smaller than the gap associated with class and 'race'. In relation to the national average, African-Caribbean pupils and their peers from unskilled manual homes experience the greatest disadvantage. The trends highlighted by this graph concur with the research by Gillborn and Mirza (2000), that:

> of the three best-known dimensions of inequality ('race', class and gender) the latter, gender, and in particular boys' underperformance, represents the narrowest disparity. In contrast to the disproportionate media attention, [our] data shows gender to be a less problematic issue than the significant disadvantage of 'race', and the even greater inequality of class.

(Gillborn and Mirza 2000, p. 23).

Furthermore, information from the Youth Cohort Study 1999, as cited by Gillborn and Mirza (op. cit.), found that although African-Caribbean, Pakistani and Bangladeshi boys are less likely to attain five higher grade GCSEs than their white or Indian peers, all 'main ethnic groups' now achieve higher attainments than ever before. This study also confirms a previous Ofsted review of research, which showed that Indian pupils as a group were the highest performing of the main South Asian categories and stated that 'they are all achieving consistently in excess of their white counterparts'.

A summary of Gillborn and Mirza's research with specific reference to the three aspects of inequality – ethnicity, social class and gender – is outlined below.

Ethnicity and attainment

- African-Caribbean, Pakistani and Bangladeshi pupils are markedly less likely to attain five higher grade GCSEs than their white and Indian peers nationally.
- White and Indian pupils are the only groups to have improving rates of attainment in each successive survey.
- Indian pupils have made the greatest gains in the last decade: enough to overtake their white peers as a group.
- Bangladeshi pupils have improved significantly but the gap between themselves and white youngsters is much the same.
- African-Caribbean and Pakistani pupils have drawn least benefit from the rising levels of attainment: the gap between them and their white peers is bigger now than a decade ago.
- Available evidence suggests that the inequalities of attainment for African-Caribbean pupils become progressively greater as they move through the school system; such differences become more pronounced between the end of primary school and the end of secondary education.

Social class and attainment

- Since the late 1980s the attainment gap between the highest and lowest social classes has widened.
- Difficulty with definitions, and the cost of analysing suitable material, means that little research gathers adequate data on social class background.
- The ways in which social class affects educational opportunities are multiple and complex: some factors lie outside the school, others operate through institutional processes that disadvantage particular groups of students.
- The familiar association between class and attainment can be seen to operate within each of the main ethnic groups.
- The majority of boys and girls from socially advantaged backgrounds do better in all subjects at GCSE than the majority of girls from disadvantaged families.
- Comparing like with like in terms of their class background, clear inequalities of attainment are evident for Pakistanis/Bangladeshi and African-Caribbean students.
- Inequalities of attainment are now evident for black students regardless of their class backgrounds.
- African-Caribbean students from manual backgrounds fell behind other working class peers in levels of attainment during the late 1980s and 1990s.

- African-Caribbean students from non-manual homes are the lowest attaining of the middle class groups. In some cases they are barely matching the attainments of working class students in other ethnic groups.

Gender and attainment

- The gender gap is considerably smaller than the inequalities of attainment associated with ethnic origin and social class background.
- In each of the principal ethnic groups nationally, girls are more likely to achieve five higher grade GCSEs than boys of the same ethnic origin.
- Ethnic inequalities persist when comparing groups of pupils of the same sex but with different ethnic origins.
- The inequalities of attainment of Bangladeshi/Pakistani and African-Caribbean girls not only mean that they do less well than white and Indian girls, they are also less likely to attain five higher grade GCSEs than white and Indian boys.
- No group has been completely excluded from the improvement in GCSE attainments during the late 1980s and 1990s.

Practical task

The following scenarios are based on actual events that have taken place. With one or more trainee teacher colleagues, discuss the issues that arise and consider what their implications are for practice.

- *A grandparent complained to the LEA that the primary school where his granddaughter attended had used a black doll to represent the baby Jesus. He had complained directly to the headteacher the previous year and felt that his concerns had been ignored. He found it unacceptable for Jesus Christ to be portrayed as black. 'I could understand it if the doll was slightly brown because we know that the Holy Land is in the Middle East and hot – so people could be a bit tanned'.*

- *Overheard in a staff room – 'I'm a white middle-aged and middle class woman; what can I possibly do to help underachieving black boys? It's just so far removed from my world.'*

- *A parent makes a complaint that two other children are bullying his 15-year-old daughter in and out of the classroom. He also reported that his daughter was having nightmares and showed extreme reluctance about going to school. He then went on to say that the daughter had recently started praying to become white.*

Strategies for addressing differences in attainment

Classroom story

The Northwards Comprehensive School data base shows that the achievement of Pakistani boys is significantly lower than the average school achievement, whereas the achievement of Pakistani girls is higher than average. In July 2001, at the end of the KS3 National Literacy Strategy pilot, concern was expressed that although all pupils progressed over Year 7, the progression of Pakistani boys was not as great as any other group. The attainment gap therefore is an issue at this early stage in a pupil's secondary education. Northwards instigated an observational study of students in English groups in Year 7 and Year 8. The observations indicated, as would be expected, a wide range of ability, achievement and motivation within the group of Pakistani boys in these two Year groups.

As a result of the observation the following actions can be initiated to possibly bring about change in outcomes for this target group.

A whole school's response may include:

- **an examination of the curriculum content to reflect the interests and prior experiences of all its students;**
- **evaluation of its teaching and learning strategies;**
- **development of whole school policies, which cover all aspects of work and behaviour.**

(The school's formally taught curriculum and the informal hidden curriculum should take into account and reflect the linguistic and cultural diversity of the school and the community it serves. The teaching and learning in school should reflect this range of diversity.)

The whole school response is aimed at creating an ethos whereby Pakistani boys can achieve without fear of ridicule. The impact of the whole school's response can then be monitored to ascertain:

- **levels of attainment and progress;**
- **levels of engagement with school life - participation in activities both in the classroom and beyond.**

For detailed guidance refer to *Learning for All: Standards for Racial Equality in Schools*, Commission for Racial Equality at **www.cre.gov.uk**

The research into achievement has mainly focused on the extent of the differences as measured through testing and examination results and the likely reasons for the differences. It has viewed achievement in narrow terms that conflate attainment with the broader concept of achievement which could be argued as attainment plus representation, participation etc, in short, social inclusion. The strategies for addressing differences in attainment have focused very much on the role of the school, whereas indicators of achievement would require greater acknowledgement of the wider societal changes in the labour market that have taken place over the past ten years or more and the impact this has had on boys' attitudes to schooling as can be gleaned from the following quote:

> The collapse of the manufacturing industry and the introduction of new technologies in the workplace have conspired to make working class boys feel useless and unwanted. The disaffection has spread to the classroom.
>
> (Martin Bright *The Observer* March 1998)

Equality and inclusion:

a summary of key points

- *The terms* equal opportunities *and* equality of opportunity *have to be informed by an understanding of the concept of* equality.

- *The concept of* inclusion, *as used in the context of education and schooling in the present political climate, refers to the role of education and its contribution to reducing disaffection and promoting participation in the political, social and economic life of wider society.*

- *Whilst girls generally may be doing well in schooling up to GCSE, they fail in later life to capitalise upon this seeming success and still end up occupying the low ranks in most areas of work, especially in the business sector.*

- *Since the late 1980s the attainment gap between the highest and lowest social classes has widened. The ways in which social class affects educational opportunities are multiple and complex: some factors lie outside the school, others operate through institutional processes that disadvantage particular groups of students.*

- *Social class and gender differences are closely associated with differences in attainment but neither can account for persistent underlying ethnic inequalities: comparing like with like, African-Caribbean, Pakistani and Bangladeshi students do not enjoy equal opportunities.*

The intention of this chapter was to make complex ideas accessible to trainee and beginner teachers unfamiliar with issues relating to equality and inclusion. It is vital that these understandings are put into practice so that they become central to your teaching and learning strategies. Promoting equality and inclusion is a cornerstone of being a member of one of the most influential professions in society.

Further reading

Epstein, D., Elwood, J., Hey, V. and Maw, J. (1998) *Failing Boys? Issues in Gender and Achievement*. Buckingham. Open University Press. This is a useful and accessible text which explores the complex issues relating to masculinity, schooling and achievement.

Gaine, C. and George, R. (1999) *Gender, 'Race' and Class in Schooling: A New Introduction*. London. Falmer Press. This book provides an overview of research and key problems in the field of education and the three social inequalities – gender, 'race' and class.

Gilborn, D. and Mirza, H. S. (2002) *Educational Inequality: Mapping 'Race', Class and Gender: A Synthesis of Research*. London. Ofsted.

Griffiths, M. (2003) *Action for Social Justice in Education: Fairly Different*. Buckingham. Open University.

Searle, C. (2001) *An Exclusive Education: 'Race', Class and Exclusion in British Schools*. London. Lawrence and Wishart. This text analyses the exclusionary practices of many secondary schools and puts forward policies to reverse this situation. It places educational exclusion within the wider context of social and political exclusion.

For further information on equality and inclusion, visit **www.learning matters. co.uk/education/learnteach/chapt11.html**

Glossary

Black is sometimes used as a general term for people of African, Caribbean, South Asian and other Asian origin. Black is also one of the ethnic monitoring categories used in the census. It includes Caribbeans, Africans and others who wish to describe themselves as black.

Ethnicity and ethnic group. Ethnicity is an unambiguous term, which refers to culture. An ethnic group is simply a group which shares certain cultural features such as language, religion, various customs, perhaps food and clothing preferences (Gaine and George 1999).

Gender refers to those characteristics of being female or male which are socially constructed.

Institutional racism. The *Stephen Lawrence Inquiry Report* defines institutional racism as:

> The collective failure of an organisation to provide an appropriate and professional service to people because of their colour, culture or ethnic origin. It can be seen or detected in processes, attitudes and behaviour which amount to discrimination through unwitting prejudice, ignorance, thoughtlessness and racist stereotyping which disadvantage minority ethnic people.

'Race' is a crude and superficial classification, which began in the last century; it has no biological significance to scientists today. Perhaps a useful working definition is 'a group of people who may share some physical characteristic to which social importance is attached'. Thus, the important facet of 'race' is not the skin colour, facial features or type of hair people have but the social significance which is placed upon these (Gaine and George op.cit.).

Racism. The *Stephen Lawrence Inquiry Report* defines racism as:

> … conduct or words which advantage or disadvantage people because of their colour, culture or ethnic origin. In its more subtle form it is as damaging as in its overt form.

Using this definition, black, white or Asian people may be victims of racism. This definition of racism is consistent with the Race Relations Act. Some groups of people (for example black people, Asians, Gypsies and asylum seekers) are much more likely to suffer racism. Racism is sometimes used to refer to the power relationship between white people and black people. The basis for this viewpoint is that white people make most of the social, economic and political decisions and that these decisions may systematically disadvantage black people. 'Black' is used politically in this context to unite people who are not white or who are likely to be subjected to racism (for example Jewish people).

Racist incident is any incident that is perceived to be racist by the victim, or any other person.

Sexism is the discrimination against women or men on the basis of their sex.

Social inclusion refers to participation in society. It includes involvement in politics and in the economy and mainstream cultural life.

12 TEACHING AS PROFESSIONAL INQUIRY: THE IMPORTANCE OF RESEARCH AND EVIDENCE

SUE BRINDLEY

Introduction

By meeting the Standards you've been reading about in this book, you'll certainly qualify to be a teacher. But is there anyone reading this who wouldn't claim to want to be not just a teacher, but a *good* teacher? That is, someone who actively thinks about teaching and learning; who wants to keep up to date with their subject; who wants to keep their enthusiasm for teaching and education. The standard quoted above is a short statement, easy to overlook – or underestimate in importance. It is this standard, however, that is going to be the hallmark of the good teacher, the critical thinker, rather than the technician, encapsulated in Donald Schön's term, 'the reflective practitioner' (Schön 1983). It's the quality which the best mentor you have worked with displayed – the ability to articulate good practice, to explain beyond the anecdotal level why strategies work in the classroom – in short, to construct a conceptual framework that allows you to transfer the knowledge from one teaching situation to another, and to know why you're choosing to do so. It is absolutely clear from the positioning of this standard in Professional Values and Practice, and the alignment with the General Teaching Council's Professional Code, that research and evidence go hand in hand with teaching as a professional activity.

Practical task

As part of this chapter, you will be encouraged to keep a research diary. You can choose to do this either electronically, or using pen and paper. The purpose of this research diary is twofold: to allow you to record your own progress as a researcher over time, and to keep a record of those articles and sources you find useful in supporting your own professional development.

Research diaries are also a useful methodological tool (see, for example, Robson 1993 pp.254-255) for any research you decide to undertake. Robson refers to diaries neither read nor seen as useful by the 'client group' of teachers. He compared teaching with the medical profession which, he pointed out, used evidence to develop practice in ways which teaching had not. (It is also worth reading Hargreaves' later address to BERA 2001 to see how his thinking developed on this theme.) Hargreaves' call to revitalise – indeed re-invent – educational research was taken up with enthusiasm by Chris Woodhead, then HMCI of Ofsted and not noted for his support of academics (or teachers, it may be said). Woodhead commissioned, ironically, research into Hargreaves' claim, appointing James Tooley, now Professor of Education Policy at the University of Newcastle Upon Tyne and then director of the training and education unit at the Institute of Economic Affairs, a right-wing think tank, to lead this. Tooley's report, some would say unsurprisingly in the light of his perceived political positioning, was highly critical of educational research (see Tooley and Darby 1998). In an incestuous move, Tooley's position was then criticised by a number of academics, not least for claimed flaws in his research methodology (see for example Goldstein 1998, Armstrong 1999).

In 1998, the DfEE commissioned the Institute for Employment Studies at the University of Sussex to produce a review of educational research. Their report (Hillage et al. 1998) called for 'more partnerships' in research and the need for 'evidence based policy'. As part of their findings, the report called for a central research body which would advise educational researchers on the needs of the education community, the 'users' of research. The proposal was that this committee would include teachers who would give the practitioners' perspective. This was an interesting development. Seemingly a pragmatic response to the identified problem of irrelevance, it nevertheless drew a warning response from Harvey Goldstein, arguing strongly on the basis of intellectual freedom in research, stating that ' ... if the recommendations of this report were to be implemented I would have very grave concerns for the future of educational research in this country' (1998). In fact, a National Educational Research Forum was set up in 1999, to advise on key areas to research in education.

A RANGE OF PERSPECTIVES

The theme of pragmatics in educational research – or centralisation and control of knowledge, depending on the ideological frame you bring to this – was developed in some sectors with enthusiasm and rapidity. The Teacher Training Agency (TTA), for example, took the theme of 'classroom focused' as their central tenet to define 'good' educational research, and used the criterion of 'raising standards' as the purpose for undertaking educational research. I want to discuss later the routes that their thinking has taken, but I think it's important to note that the research commissioned by agencies such as the TTA is just one representation of educational research. As trainee teachers, you will want to engage with a range of perspectives, not least so that you are able to distinguish and select from a range of research positions, and to understand the principles that underpin that research and thus to become 'research critically literate' – able to explore the production of knowledge and test its claims to authenticity.

as 'a kind of self administered questionnaire' and it may be helpf
description as a starting point.

- *Design a research diary. Ensure you have a section to record your*
  of becoming a researcher, and one which will allow you to record
  evidence you discover during your own research. Using research y
  already undertaken for an assignment, record your first diary entr

Evidence

What do the standards mean by evidence? In terms of teaching in 2002 and beyon
encapsulates a thrust of thinking that challenges teaching to become 'an evide
based profession'. Teachers are exhorted to use educational research to inform pr
tice, with the associated agenda of 'raising standards' ever present. But
apparently straightforward link carries with it a constellation of issues.

The debates

The area, and indeed the legitimisation of educational research, is fiercely conteste
and debated. A brief, recent history may serve to give you the flavour of this.

It was perhaps Stenhouse who first gave the notion of teacher as researcher rea
currency. In 1975, in his book *An Introduction to Curriculum Research and Development*,
he argued that 'a research tradition which is accessible to teachers and which feeds
teaching must be created if education is to be significantly improved'. The role of the
teacher was that of active researcher.

The idea of teachers exploring their own practice then became enshrined in Schön's
'reflective practitioner' where the good teacher was the teacher who evaluated their
teaching either through 'knowledge in action' or 'reflection in action' (Schön 1983).

Where teachers (and schools) took up these ideas in practice it was often through
action research – an approach first described by Kurt Lewin (1946) and which has as
its methodology a cycle of planning, acting, observing and reflecting. Action research
has become a significant way for teachers to incorporate research into their teaching,
with a focus on improvement:

> ... firstly, the improvement of a practice of some kind; secondly, the improvement
> of the situation in which practice takes place those involved in the practice being
> considered are to be involved in the action research process in all its aspects.
>
> (Carr and Kemmis 1986, p. 165)

Other views

Things were livened up by David Hargreaves, then Professor of Education at the
University of Cambridge, and subsequently Chief Executive of QCA, in his address to
the Teacher Training Agency (1996). Hargreaves was addressing primarily the 'professional researchers' and claimed that educational research lacked rigour, and was

Practical task

In your research diary, record your own views and experiences, if any, on the purposes and potential of research in education. You might like to consider:

- *the place of research in your own subject area;*
- *the place of research in your own professional development;*
- *the views of those already involved in the debate (as outlined above, and others you may want to call upon).*

Add a record of any other readings you have discovered on the place of research in education, and in your own subject area.

Research – when?

The temptation with pressures of time, both now in your training period and in your equally busy career as a teacher, is that you will be seduced by the 'what works *now* in my classroom' approach to research. I do not want to deny the place of such explorations. But I want to extend this, and to do so in an appeal to the notion of professionalism. In a longitudinal project currently being undertaken in my own institution, led by Professor Donald McIntyre and looking at the developing expertise of beginning teachers (DEBT Project), two major reasons given by trainee teachers for coming in to teaching are:

- **a desire to continue to be engaged with the subject;**
- **and an interest in how children learn.**

In interviews we conducted later in their careers, it became clear that these interests were still present – in fact were stronger. But there is also evidence that the teachers often cannot pursue these central concerns. Instead they have become marooned on an island of 'busyness' where time to develop their own thinking has become low priority in the onslaught of 'things to do'. My own research on 'Becoming an English Teacher', undertaken with my colleague Jackie Manuel at the University of Western Sydney, echoes these findings where teachers we have interviewed in both the UK and Australia say the same thing – we want to do this, but where's the time? It's a legitimate cry. But we also know that a parallel statement from teachers is that they're being asked to do more and more – and somehow, they do. They 'make' the time to administer more, or mark more, or teach more. So it's not simply about time (though nobody in their right mind would claim teachers have enough) – it's about *legitimising time to research,* that is, seeing research as something which is important enough to prioritise in the welter of day to day tasks. And to see it in this way because, as Ruddock (2001) says:

> At a time when teachers' work has intensified, when there are more bureaucratic pressures, you might expect teacher research to be pushed aside. But instead it is flourishing. It flourishes, I think because research leads teachers back to the things that lie at the heart of their professionalism, *pupils, teaching, and learning.*
>
> (Ruddock 2001)

Well, why – and how?

Recently I interviewed a series of teachers who had chosen to become involved in school based small scale research projects. I wanted to know why they had chosen to spend (or legitimise) time exploring areas of teaching in this way. I had expected replies to refer to promotions or school development plans. Whatever their original motivation, the teachers I interviewed virtually all expressed surprise at their own findings about this; that the greatest pleasure – indeed the almost addictive pleasure to be found in research – was the return to being a learner:

> Emma: I've been in teaching four years – this is coming up to my fifth, and I'd forgotten what a buzz I get from being a learner. It's funny, isn't it, that my job's about learning – I'm constantly telling the kids, students, to concentrate on their learning or to think about their learning or whatever, but it's taken this [her research project] to remind me that I really enjoy learning. I used to go home and perhaps moan about this or that to my partner – but now he can't stop me talking about this work. I love it, I just love finding me again.

> Paul: When I took this on, mainly because you made me, I really didn't think there'd be any value in it at all. Couldn't see the point of wasting valuable time reading all that stuff about what others knew about teaching. I've been teaching for years – what were they going to say that was new? But to my own surprise, well, shock, in fact, I've become caught by the research. As I'm teaching, I catch myself thinking differently about the reactions of the students, and classifying them, for God's sake! I feel like I'm learning abut teaching in ways I'd forgotten I could. I feel energised by it.

I want to use this evidence about teachers as learners in relation to both using and undertaking research.

A staging frame

The 'How' question takes us a bit further in thinking about the significance of the demands of the standards. If, for the purposes of this chapter, we use a broad definition of research as concerned with the creation and development of knowledge, involving a systematic collection of evidence framed around a question and mapped against existing knowledge, we can see that it is a demanding activity.

What I should like to suggest here is a 'staging framework' for describing ways of responding to the Standard 1.7 as a trainee teacher.

The first stage we might term 'exploration', reflecting the distinction made between using and doing research.

Exploration

As trainee teachers, it is likely that you will 'use' research findings – to support your own assignment writing, to develop ideas of your own in your teaching area, or perhaps in another construction of research – curriculum development – to research materials for your own lesson plans.

In the 'exploration' stage you will be examining the findings and ways in which others in the field have mapped this area. In practical terms, you are likely to have found this information in education journals, either in the library or online. You may well have undertaken a search around a particular area using methods, although probably not sources, familiar to you from your degree course. Part of the work you will be doing here is to establish which sources are going to be of particular use to you: some deal with diverse issues related to education, some specialise in particular areas. It is through reading and building knowledge of these sources that you will begin to build a concept map of key issues, key thinkers and key developments. It will also begin to reveal where the tensions and gaps are in knowledge and where you, as a developing professional, might be able to contribute to the knowledge base in your field.

Reading and sourcing research: practical advice

If you are as yet inexperienced in using research, you might find it helpful to have the following guidelines:

READING

In a sense, this is almost a skimming and scanning activity, though of a particular type. In the first instance, you will be building a range of resources to read and you will need to undertake rapid first evaluations of how useful a text may be. Rather than attempting to speed-read the whole article, read the abstract (if there is one) and the conclusion. Note keywords if there are any printed at the beginning of the article, a convention with some journals; look at the bibliography and note any names that recur over a number of articles – you will begin to build a picture of those who are the central participants in that debate. If an article looks useful, read the first (topic) sentence of each paragraph. If it's well written, this will allow you to see the key ideas that are explored in depth within the article. After filtering out a number of articles this way, you will be able to spend time sensibly on reading in-depth articles directly useful to you. It's likely by now that you will have developed your own note taking style – but if you haven't, try simply writing a sentence on each key paragraph, noting down the central idea. Most importantly, when you do use a text, record author, title, date and publisher, or web source. 'Endnote' is a useful piece of software to record sources and quotations if you have access to that, or simply use library index cards. Spending hours on trying to find that useful quote from a pile of papers is frustrating and hugely time consuming.

SOURCING

Two major sources for written texts are libraries and online references. It is likely that you will have the facility in your library to consult research databases – collections of articles, papers, books that have been published and which the library can usually source for you through inter-library loans if they are not available on the library shelves. Two commonly used databases are BEI (British Education Index) and ERIC (Educational Resources Information Centre). Although straightforward to use, you will almost certainly need a password, so the library is the first stop here. For simple online searches, you could simply use a search engine such as Google at **www.google. com** and enter key words to take you to articles. However, two caveats should be borne in mind.

- The keyword selection is critical. You need to be as specific as possible, and be prepared to narrow down your search if you find you have entered a word such as 'numeracy' which will source literally thousands of articles. Think carefully and precisely about the exact aspect you want to read about (numeracy+ICT). Similarly, it is all too easy to follow interesting but fundamentally unproductive (for your current purposes) lines of enquiry as you proceed through the articles that the search engine has identified. This is electronic displacement activity – don't let it lull you into thinking it is useful!

- The second caveat refers to provenance of text: there is no control over publication on the Internet – and so no guarantee that what you find there is valid or worth your while reading. Unless you know the source, it's probably best to avoid quoting from such articles as if they were seminal texts.

Perhaps a more secure route is to access education journals, including those from your own professional organisations, online. Again, you can use a search engine with the name of a journal and keywords for your research. You will find that increasing numbers of publishers have online versions of their journals that you can access. There are still some who require subscription either from you as an individual or from your library, so it is worth checking with your library about that aspect.

Indeed, librarians themselves are invaluable when it comes to sourcing information. They will know not only the larger sources of information such as those mentioned here, but also the more local resources you can use. It is always wise to use the librarians themselves as a resource.

As a final note, just as you should consider the provenance of text on the Internet, you need to consider the provenance of research when you read reports. It is worth establishing whose needs are served by the published work and who funded that work. It can – although it shouldn't in the spirit of 'pure' research – impact on what is reported and what, often more significantly, is left unsaid.

Government sources

Government publications and websites offer a significant range of evidence that you should use to inform your own research. Many of the major government agencies now address the concept of research and evidence directly. In this section, I want to direct your attention to five main sources of research and evidence.

TEACHER TRAINING AGENCY (TTA)

The TTA's own view of their function in terms of research is to be found under their REIP (Promoting Research and Evidence-Informed Practice) page, where they state:

> The TTA is active in supporting the Government in its drive to promote teaching as a research and evidence-informed profession as a means of improving teaching and learning and raising standards... It aims to influence both the supply and demand for research and evidence with and on behalf of teachers.

The TTA's agenda for educational research which has a focus on the promotion of teachers as researchers. Inevitably, there is a political gloss to this based on the 'user-producer/user-consumption' view of research (for alternative views see, for example, Hammersley 1993) and on making research 'useful'.

Nevertheless, the work being undertaken by the TTA is a valuable source of information for teachers. You might want to look for example at Jean Ruddock's Opening Address for the DfES and TTA Conference (March 2001: **www.canteach.gov.uk/ research**) where she talks of the 'quiet revolution':

> ... in teacher research we have a grass roots movement, building up slowly over the years, gradually gaining recognition and national legitimacy. It is a remarkable achievement – a quiet revolution.
>
> (Ruddock 2001)

and link Ruddock's view to the research reports generated by teachers as part of the DfES sponsored Best Practice Research Scholarships (see **www.dfes.gov.uk**). These small scale research reports were examples of classroom focused work, often based on action research projects, and demonstrate the range and quality of research being undertaken in schools. An interesting development has been the introduction of Pupils as Researchers in some schools (see, for example, Sharnbrook Upper School, seminar 27, DfES and TTA Conference 2001: Using Research and Evidence to improve teaching and learning). Unfortunately, and for reasons that are unclear, the BPRS scheme has come to an end.

DEPARTMENT FOR EDUCATION AND SKILLS (DfES)
The DfES is a valuable source of research information. The website **www.teachernet. gov.uk** has an outline of research currently being undertaken and information on research opportunities in education. At the time of writing, the website outlines its intentions thus:

> You can find out how to become involved in research, find out about research networks, access publications and articles and get hold of the latest statistics as well as discover sources of useful information on education systems in other countries.

Potentially, this is a useful site for research and evidence and one worth noting.

OFFICE FOR STANDARDS IN EDUCATION (Ofsted)
The third government resource for research and evidence is Ofsted. The database of information on schools held by Ofsted is extensive. Although they do not have a dedicated research area on the website, there are publications that form a research database. Part of using research in a professional capacity in teaching is accessing and interpreting external statistical information and Ofsted's national statistical base is probably not equalled elsewhere in the UK.

QUALIFICATIONS AND CURRICULUM AGENCY (QCA)

QCA styles its research centre as 'research and statistical information'. They define their approach as 'research and statistical analysis, [with] evaluation activities support [ing QCA's] efforts to develop effective policies to raise achievement and improve learning'. A range of publications available through the website at **www.qca.gov.uk** extend the evidence base available.

BRITISH EDUCATIONAL COMMUNICATIONS AND TECHNOLOGY AGENCY (Becta)

Becta focuses on ICT in education. Its research and evidence aim is to 'engage in a range of evidence-gathering activities regarding the use and impact of information and communications technology (ICT) in education' and it does this through a series of projects. A useful source is the ICT Research Network which 'seeks to encourage the exchange of information between all those with an interest in research on ICT in education, in order to inform the national agenda and professional practice'. This site also welcomes contributions from teachers on ICT and research.

NATIONAL FOUNDATION FOR EDUCATIONAL RESEARCH (NFER)

Whilst not government funded, an additional UK and international source which you should be aware of is the National Foundation for Educational Research. NFER undertakes research for government but also for a wide range of other users.
The website (**www.nfer.ac.uk**) offers a comprehensive overview of current and completed research both UK and internationally based. They define their work as:

> Improving education and training nationally and internationally by undertaking research, development and dissemination activities and by providing information services... by being the leading independent educational research institution in the UK, with a diversified portfolio of research, information and development activities that spans all sectors of education and training.

Of particular use is the comprehensive book list to be found on current topics of research. You can access this at **www.nfer.ac.uk/infoservices/hot.topics.asp** NFER can also be contacted directly via the website.

There are of course an almost infinite number and range of resources to support this stage of exploration. Those discussed here are a beginning point for your own research activity. The next section asks you to consider how.

How? A research 'thinking frame'

Perhaps one of the most striking discoveries identified by the trainees and teachers with whom I work is the mindframe of enthusiasm for exploring education that researching activity generates. After all, it's likely that you came into teaching precisely because you enjoyed thinking about your subject area. That intellectual curiosity is a key part of professionalism. Stale teaching often reflects stale thinking and as a professional, it's a part of your job to draw students in by demonstrating your own ongoing interest in the field. It links to the quality that has emerged time and again in the DEBT project in response to the question 'what makes a good teacher'– the answer given is enthusiasm. This powerful characteristic is a way of thinking. It is about excitement in exploring knowledge and about wanting to share that excitement. So the activity of engaging with research is valuable in itself – the intellectual energy created through discovery and the rigour of organising the knowledge gained into relevant frameworks. The teachers quoted earlier, Emma and Paul, draw us back into the idea of teachers as learners – and the strengths to be found in this positioning.

Generating and networking research

> … access to ideas that enable people to conceptualise alternatives are crucial to learning.
>
> (Young and Lucas 1999)

This section is really a glimpse into the future. You are indeed a rarity if as a trainee teacher you have the opportunity to engage with research beyond the exploration stage or small-scale assignment level work, so I am going to extend the 'increasing' part of the reference in the Standard 1.7 'tak(ing) increasing responsibility for their own professional development' into your career post initial training. This bridging move makes sense too in terms of the Career Entry Profile, a document designed to ensure continuity between your training and your year as a newly qualified teacher (NQT), and the implicit assumption that the PGCE year isn't the end of your training. Perhaps it's where teacher education begins instead.

Generating and Networking Research is the stage where exploration begins to shade from 'using' into an active approach to research. It is also arguably where you begin to make the links between 'theory' and 'practice' through the application of ideas to classroom practice. Generating research is really about developing your own identity as a researcher. It may be that during your training year you have found yourself intrigued or excited by an area of teaching and learning that you have not had the time to pursue but which now could form the basis of a profitable area for action research. It may be the type of research which the current Best Practice Research Scholarships support: small scale, classroom focused, extending over a year. It may well form the focus for you as a professional to contribute to what Calderhead (1987) refers to as 'a body of specialised knowledge acquired through training and experience'.

A research example

The type of research I am thinking of here is exemplified through the work of Rachel, who, like Paul and Emma, is also a teacher researcher. Rachel is in charge of Key Stage 2/3 transition and, following some preparatory reading, was interested to see whether the experience of English by Year 6 pupils was the same as that of Year 7 pupils. The research is still in progress, but she chose to record, over a short period of time, parallel classroom activities in English in a partner primary school and in her own secondary school, and then to interview teachers and pupils about what they thought constituted 'English'. It seems to be emerging that English in the primary school she is working with has ceased to exist and 'literacy' has taken its place. When pupils come into the secondary school, they encounter a subject whose name is familiar, but where the content is largely text based. Unfinished as it is, it is still possible to predict that Rachel's research will supply an interesting insight into pupil transfer, progression and achievement for her department to use to inform planning.

Practical task

In your research diary, note areas emerging from your PGCE work which would be of interest to you to begin to research in your early years of teaching. Ensure that you transfer these to your CEP for discussion with your induction tutor.

Plan to develop your identity as a researcher, and to make it an integral part of your own professional development. Use the research you plan to discuss with your induction tutor as the beginning of this process. Share your findings with colleagues either informally through departmental meetings, or more formally through CPD days, or in due course, by contributing to conferences and by publication.

Continue to use the diary over this time. At the end of each term, review how your views and experiences of research have changed. You will discover that the diary will form a valuable record of your own professional development.

Networking

Associated with the generating stage is that of 'networking' knowledge, that is, the linking together of generated research projects to contribute to that notion of a 'community of practice' (Lave and Wenger 1996). Briefly, this theory states that 'real life' learning takes place in a necessary context: 'situated learning'. They go on to propose, however, that 'legitimate peripheral participation' means that people learn by participating in 'communities of practice': that not just the individual learns through engaging in specific activities, but the whole community learns. Networking research records and establishes that learning. Building understanding in teaching is about being active in bringing about a community of learners and expanding the community of practice that is part of being a profession. This is the area which should feature in the next stage of your own professional development, not as a further 'task' but as part of the pleasure of being a teacher.

I am going to let Emma have the last word:

> I don't think I could have anticipated the impact this research has had on me. I don't think about just teaching any more – I think about education. I belong to this community still (department and school) but to a wider community too – the research community. I just feel like I'm learning so much and it's good. It really is good.

Further reading

Guides to undertaking educational research

Hart, C. (1998) *Doing a Literature Review*. London. Sage. A useful, practical guide to producing a formal account and analysis of existing literature in the field. Examples at the end of each chapter. Sample contents list includes classifying and reading research, argumentation analysis, organising and expressing ideas, mapping and analysing ideas.

Hitchcock, G. and Hughes, D. (1995) *Research and the Teacher*. London. Routledge. Written for practising teachers, focusing on qualitative research. Helpful section on designs and approaches.

Hopkins, D. (2002) *A Teacher's Guide to Classroom Research*. Buckingham. Open University Press. A good overview with a strongly practical approach to researching in the classroom.

Robson, R. (1993) *Real World Research*. Oxford. Blackwell. A comprehensive, and comprehensible, guide to research methodology.

Useful journals

There are a range of subject specific and general educational journals. For particular reference to research issues, you might try:

AERA (American Educational Research Association): publishes a number of journals which focus on education and research (see **www.aera.net**). A very good source for accessing research beyond the UK perspective.

British Educational Research Journal (BERJ): Carfax (see also **www.bera.ac.uk** for details of conferences). Well known and well respected journal which focuses largely, but not exclusively, on educational research in the UK. This is the journal of the British Educational Research Association (BERA) which holds annual conferences, usually in September.

Educational Research Abstracts: Taylor and Francis (online). Useful overview via abstracts of current research in education.

Educational Action Research: *Triangle Journal* which focuses on both the methodology of action research and articles exemplifying this approach.

For further information on teaching as professional inquiry, visit **www.learning matters. co.uk/education/learnteach/chaptl2.html**

Allen, J., Loveless, A., Potter, J. and Sharp, J. (2000) *Primary ICT: Knowledge, Understanding and Practice*. Exeter. Learning Matters.

Assessment Reform Group (1999) *Assessment for Learning: Beyond the Black Box*. Cambridge. University of Cambridge School of Education.

Barbe, W. B. and Malone, M.N. (1981) What we know about modelling strategies. *Educational Leadership*, 38, 378-80.

Barratt, R. and Barratt Hacking, E. (2000) Changing my locality: conceptions of the future. *Teaching Geography*, 25(1), 17-21.

Barrs, M. (1990) *Words Not Numbers: Assessment in English*. Exeter. Short Run Press.

Basic Skills Agency (1997) *Does Numeracy Matter? Evidence from the National Child Development Study on the Impact of Poor Numerary on Adult Life*.

Bassey, M. (1989) *Teaching Practice in the Primary School*. East Grinstead. Ward Lock Educational.

Beard, R. (1993) *Teaching Literacy Balancing Perspectives*. London. Routledge.

Beard, R. (2000) *Developing Writing 3-13*. London. Hodder and Stoughton.

Bearne, E. (1999) *Use of Language Across the Secondary Curriculum*. London. Routledge.

Becta (2001) *ImpaCT2*. Norwich. HMSO.

Becta (2001) The secondary school of the future. A preliminary report to DfEE by Becta **www.becta.org.uk/news/reports/secondaryfuture/**

Behets, D. (1990) Concerns of pre-service physical education teachers. *Journal of Teaching in Physical Education*, 10, 66-75.

Bereiter, C. and Scardamalia, M. (1987) The psychology of written composition, in Beard, R. (1993) *Teaching Literacy Balancing Perspectives*. London. Routledge.

Black, P. and Wiliam, D. (1998) *Inside the Black Box: Raising Standards Through Classroom Assessment*. London. King's College.

Bruner, J. S. (1966) *The Process of Education*. New York. Vintage.

Bruner, J. S. (1966) *Toward a Theory of Instruction*. Cambridge, MA. Harvard University Press.

Cairney, T. H. (1995) *Pathways to Literacy*. London. Cassell.

Calderhead, J. (1987) *Exploring Teachers' Thinking*. London. Cassell.

Cano-Garcia, F. and Hughes, E.H. (2000) Learning and thinking styles: an analysis of their interrelationship and influences on academic achievement. *Educational Psychology*, 20(4), 413-430.

Capel, S., Leask, M. and Turner, T. (1995) *Learning to Teach in the Secondary School*. London. Routledge.

Carr, W. and Kemmis, S. (1986) *Becoming Critical*. London. Falmer Press.

Chasty, H. (1990) cited in P. D. Pumfrey and C. D. Elliott (eds.) (1990) *Children's Difficulties in Reading, Spelling and Writing*. London. Falmer Press.

Cheminais, R. (2000) *Special Educational Needs for Newly Qualified and Student Teachers*. London. David Fulton.

Child, D. (1986) *Psychology and the Teacher* (4th ed.). London. Cassell.

Cole, M. (ed.) (1999) *Professional Issues for Teachers and Student Teachers*. London. David Fulton.

Cotton, J. (1995) *The Theory of Learners: An Introduction*. London. Kogan Page.

Counsell, C. (2001) Challenges facing the literacy co-ordinator, in *Literacy Today*, 24.

Cowley, S. (2001) *Getting the Buggers to Behave*. London. Continuum.

Dean, G. (2000) *Teaching Literacy in Secondary Schools*. London. David Fulton.

DES (1978) *Special Educational Needs: Warnock Report*. London. HMSO.

DES (1981) *Education Act*. London. HMSO.

DfEE (1995) *Disability Discrimination Act*. London. HMSO.

DfEE (1996) *Education Act*. London. HMSO.

DfEE (1997) *Excellence for All Children: Meeting Special Educational Needs* (Green Paper). London. HMSO.

DfEE (1997) *Excellence in Schools*. Cm 3681. London. HMSO.

DfEE (1998) *Meeting Special Educational Needs: A Programme of Action*. London. HMSO.

DfEE (1999) *Social Inclusion: Pupil Support*. Circular 10/99. London. HMSO.

DfEE (2001) *Framework for Teaching English: Years 7, 8 and 9*. DfEE.

DfEE (2001) *Key Stage 3 National Strategy Framework for Teaching Mathematics: Years 7, 8 and 9*.

DfEE (2001) *Literacy Across the Curriculum*. DfEE.

DfEE (1999) A fresh start – improving literacy and numeracy skills. *Skills and Enterprise Briefing*, Issue 5/99.

DfEE and QCA (2000) *The National Curriculum for England*. DfEE and QCA Publications.

DfES (2001) *Numeracy Across the Curriculum Notes for School-Based Training*.

DfES (2001) *Numeracy Across the Curriculum Support Materials for School-Based Training*.

DfES (2001) *Schools Achieving Success*. White Paper. HMSO.

DfES (2001) *Special Educational Needs and Disability Act*. Nottingham. DfES Publications.

DfES (2001) *Special Educational Needs: Code of Practice*. Nottingham. DfES Publications.

DfES (2002) *Qualifying to Teach*: Professional Standards for Qualified Teacher Status and Requirements for Initial Teacher Training (online). Available from **www.canteach.gov.uk/itt/requirements/qualifying/standards_printable.pdf**

DfES (2002) *Transforming the Way We Learn*. Norwich. HMSO.

Dodds, P., Griffin, L. L. and Placek, J. H. (2001) A selected review of the literature on the development of learners' domain-specific knowledge. *Journal of Teaching in Physical Education*, 20(4), 301-313.

Doyle, W. (1979) Classroom tasks and student's abilities, in P. Peterson and H. Walberg (eds.) *Research on Teaching: Concepts, Findings and Implications*. 183–209. Berkeley, CA. McCutcheon.

Doyle, W. (1981) Research on classroom contexts. *Journal of Teacher Education*, 32(6): 3–6.

Driscoll, M.P. (1994) *Psychology for Learning*. Needham Heights, MA. Allyn and Bacon.

Ellis, V. with High, S. (2004) Something more to tell you: gay, lesbian or bisexual young people's experiences of schooling, *British Educational Research Journal*, 30(2): 213–225.

Emig, J. (1977) Writing as a mode of learning. *College Composition and Communication* 28(2): 122-128.

Epstein, D., Elwood, J., Hey, V. and Maw, J. (1998) *Failing Boys? Issues in Gender and Achievement*. Buckingham. Open University Press.

Felder, R.M. and Silverman, L.K. (1988) Learning and teaching styles in engineering education. *Engineering Education*, April, 674-680.

Fuller, F. F. (1969) Concerns of teachers: a developmental conceptualisation. *American Educational Research Journal*, 70, 263-8.

Gaine, C. and George, R. (1999) *Gender, 'Race' and Class in Schooling: A New Introduction*. London. Falmer Press.

Galili, I. and Bar, V. (1997) Children's operational knowledge about weight. *International Journal of Science Education*, 19, 317-340.

Gardner, H. (1983) *Frames of Mind: The Theory of Multiple Intelligences*. New York. Basic Books Inc.

General Medical Council Standards of Practice. Available from **www.gmc-uk.org/ standards/standards.frameset.htm**

Gillborn, D. and Mirza, H. S. (2000) *Educational Inequality: Mapping Race, Class and Gender*. London. Ofsted.

Gipps, C. and McGilchrist, B. (1999) Primary school learners. In P. Mortimore (ed.) *Understanding Pedagogy and its Impact on Learning*. London. Paul Chapman.

Gipps. C. and Stobart, G. (1997) *Assessment: A Teacher's Guide to the Issues*. London. Hodder and Stoughton.

Glaser, R. (1976) Components of a psychology of instruction: toward a science of design. *Review of Educational Research* 46(1): 1-24.

Glaser, R. (1984) Education and thinking: the role of knowledge. *American Psychologist* 39(2): 93-104.

Goldstein, H. (1998) Response papers on **www.ioe.ac.uk/hgoldstn/**

Goleman, D. (1996) *Emotional Intelligence*. London. Bloomsbury.

Graff, H. J. (1987) *The Labyrinths of Literacy*. London. The Falmer Press.

Gredler, M.E. (2001) *Learning and Instruction: Theory into Practice* (4th ed.). New York. HarperCollins.

Griffin, L. L., Dodds, P., Placek, J. H. and Tremino, F. (2001). Middle school students' conceptions of soccer: their solutions to tactical problems. *Journal of Teaching in Physical Education*, 20(4), 324-340.

Griffiths, M. (2003) *Action for Social Justice in Education: Fairly Different*. Buckingham. Open University.

GTCE Professional Code for Teachers. Available from **www.gtce.org.uk/gtcinfo/ code.asp**

Guide to the Professional Conduct of Solicitors. Available from **www.guide-on-line.lawsociety.org.uk/**

Hammersley, M. (1993) On the teacher as researcher. *Educational Action Research*, 1(3).

Hargreaves, D. (1996) *Teaching as a Research Based Profession: Possibilities and Prospects*. London. Teacher Training Agency.

Hargreaves, D. (2001) The Nuttall Memorial/Carfax Lecture. BERA. 2001.

Harlen, W., Gipps, C., Broadfoot P. and Nuttall, D. (1994) Assessment and the Improvement of Education in A. Pollard and J. Bourne, *Teaching Learning in the Primary School*. London. Routledge.

Hart, C. (1998) *Doing a Literature Review*. London. Sage.

Haydon, G. (1996) Should teachers have their own professional ethics? *Journal of Philosophy of Education*, 30(2), 301-306.

Heffler, B. (2001) Individual learning style and the learning style inventory. *Educational Studies*, 27(3), 307-316.

Hill, D. and Cole, M. (eds.) (1999) *Promoting Equality in Secondary School*. London. Cassell.

Hillage, J., Pearson, R., Anderson, A. and Tamkin, P. (1998) *Excellence in Research in Schools*. London. DfEE.

Hitchcock, G. and Hughes, D. (1995) *Research and the Teacher*. London. Routledge.

Honey, P. and Mumford, A. (1982) *The Manual of Learning Styles*. Maidenhead. Peter Honey.

Hopkins, D. (1993) *A Teacher's Guide to Classroom Research*. Buckingham. Open University Press.

Jasmine, J. (1996) *Teaching with Multiple Intelligences*. Westminster, CA. Teacher Created Materials.

Katz, L. G. (1972) Developmental stages of preschool teachers. *Elementary School Journal*, 73(1): 50–54.

Koehn, D. (1994) *The Ground of Professional Ethics*. London. Routledge.

Kohl, H. (1986) *On Becoming a Teacher*. London. Methuen.

Kolb, D. A. (1976) *Teaching Students Through Their Individual Learning Styles*. Reston, VA. Reston Publications.

Kolb, D. A. (1984) *Experiential Learning: Experience as a Source of Learning and Development*. Englewood Cliffs, NJ. Prentice-Hall.

Kolb, D.A. (1985) *Learning Styles Inventory and Technical Manual*. Boston, MA. McBer.

Kyriacou, C. (1998) *Essential Teaching Skills* (2nd ed.). Cheltenham. Stanley Thornes.

Kyriacou, C. and Stephens, P. (1999) Student teacher concerns during teaching practice. *Evaluation and Research in Education* 13(1), 18-31.

Lave, J. (1988) *Cognition in Practice: Mind, Mathematics, and Culture in Everyday Life*. Cambridge. Cambridge University Press.

Lave, J. and Wenger, E. (1996) *Situated Learning*. Cambridge. Cambridge University Press.

Ledwick, M. (2001) *Numeracy Across the Curriculum in Secondary Schools*. Leicester. Mathematical Association.

Lewin, K. (1946) Action research and minority problems. *Journal of Social Issues*, 2, 34-6. 286, 438.

Lewis, M. and Wray, D. (2001) Implementing effective literacy strategies in the secondary school. *Educational Studies*, (27)1.

Long, M. (2000) *The Psychology of Education*. London. Routledge.

Luke, A. (1999) Education 2010 and new times: why equity and social justice matter, but differently. Paper presented at Education Queensland conference October 1999. Available from **http://education/qld.gov.au/corporate/newsbasics/ docs/onlineal.doc**

Lunzer, E. and Gardner, K. (1984) *Learning from the Written Word*. Edinburgh. Oliver & Boyd.

Marlowe, B. A. and Page, M. L. (1998) *Creating and Sustaining a Constructivist Classroom*. Thousand Oaks, CA. Sage Publications.

Medwell, J. et al. (1998) *Effective Teachers of Literacy* in M. Lewis and D. Wray (2001) Implementing effective literacy strategies in the secondary school. *Educational Studies*, (27)1.

Meek, M. (1991) *On Being Literate*. London. Bodley Head.

Monk, M. (2001) Learning in the classroom, in J. Dillon and M. Maguire (eds.) *Becoming a Teacher: Issues in Secondary Teaching*. Buckingham. Open University Press.

Montgomery, D. (1989) *Managing Behaviour Problems*. London. Hodder and Stoughton.

Morgan, C. and Morris, G. (1999) *Good Teaching and Learning*. Buckingham. Open University Press.

Moseley, D., Higgins S. et al. (1999) *Ways forward with ICT: Effective Pedagogy Using ICT for Literacy and Numeracy in Primary Schools*. Newcastle University.

Mujis, D. and Reynolds, D. (2001) *Effective Teaching: Evidence and Practice*. London. Paul Chapman Publishing.

Myhill, D. (2000) Misconceptions and difficulties in the acquisition of metalinguistic knowledge. *Learning and Education*, 14(3), 151-163.

Myhill, D. (2001) *Better Writing*. Westley. Courseware Publications.

Ofsted (1995) *Physical Education and Sport in Schools: A Survey of Good Practice*. London. HMSO.

Ofsted (2000) *Evaluating Educational Inclusion: Guidance for Inspectors and Schools*. London. Ofsted.

Ofsted (2002) *Good Teaching, Effective Departments*. London. Ofsted.

Ofsted (2004) *Standards and Quality 2002/3: The Annual Report of Her Majesty's Chief Inspector of Schools*. London. Ofsted.

Palmer, D. (2001) Students' conceptions and scientifically acceptable conceptions about gravity. *International Journal of Science Education*, 23(7), 691-706.

Papert, S. (1980) *Mindstorms: Children, Computers and Powerful Ideas*. Brighton. Harvester Press.

Pendry, A., Atha, J., Carden, S., Courtney, L., Keogh, C. and Ruston, K. (1997) Pupils' preconceptions of history. *Teaching History*, 86, 18-20.

Perks, P. and Prestage, S. (2001) *Teaching the National Numeracy Strategy at Key Stage 3*. London. David Fulton.

Phillips, D. C. and Soltis, J. (1998) *Perspectives on Learning*. New York. Columbia University.

Placek, J. H., Griffin, L. L., Dodds, P., Raymond, C., Tremino, F. and James, A. (2001) Middle school students' conceptions of fitness: A long road to a healthy lifestyle. *Journal of Teaching in Physical Education*, 20(4), 3 14-323.

Pope, S. and Sharma, R. (2001) Symbol sense: teachers' and students' understanding, in *Proceedings of the British Society for Research into Learning Mathematics*, 21(3), 64-69.

Porth Junior School (2000) Porth Junior School YEAR2KMAG (online). Available from **www.geocities.comtyear2kmag/**

QCA (1998) *ICT Across the Curriculum. An Overview*. Norwich. HMSO.

QCA (1998) *Supporting and Target Setting Process: Guidance for Effective Target Setting for Pupils with Special Educational Needs*. London. DfEE/QCA.

QCA (1999) *Information and Communication Technology. The National Curriculum for England*. Norwich. HMSO.

QCA (2000) *Language for Learning in Key Stage 3*. QCA.

QCA (2001) *Language at Work in Lessons*. QCA.

Richardson, R. and Wood, A. (1999) *Inclusive Society: Race and Identity on the Agenda*. Report produced for Race on the Agenda in partnership with Association of London Government and Save the Children. Stoke on Trent. Trentham.

Riding, R. J. and Raynor, S. G. (1998) *Cognitive Styles and Learning Strategies: Understanding Style Differences in Learning and Behaviour*. London. David Fulton.

Rink, J. E. (2001) Investigating the assumptions of pedagogy. *Journal of Teaching in Physical Education*, 20, 112-128.

Roblyer, M. D. (1996) The constructivist/objectivist debate: implications for instructional technology research. *Learning and Leading with Technology*, 24: 12–16.

Robson, R. (1993) *Real World Research*. Oxford. Blackwell.

Roelofs, E. and Terwel, J. (1999) Constructivism and authentic pedagogy: state of the art and recent developments in the Dutch national curriculum in secondary education. *Journal of Curriculum Studies*, 31(2), 201-227.

Rogers, B. (1997) *You Know the Fair Rule*. London. Prentice Hall.

Ruddock, J. (2001) The Quiet Revolution: Opening address for the DfES and TTA conference, using research and evidence to improve teaching and learning.

Sarason, S. B. (1993) *You Are Thinking of Teaching? Opportunities, Problems, Realities*. San Francisco. Jossey-Bass.

Sarason, S. B. and D. J. (1979) *Educational Handicap, Public Policy and Social History*. London. Macmillan.

Schön, D. (1983) *The Reflective Practitioner*. London. Temple Smith.

Schunk, D. H. (1996) *Learning Theories* (2nd ed.). Englewood Cliffs, NJ. Prentice Hall.

Searle, C. (2001) *An Exclusive Education: 'Race', Class and Exclusion in British Schools*. London. Lawrence and Wishart.

Secondary Heads Association (2001) *14 and Beyond: Proposals for the Development of a Coherent Post-14 Education Framework*. Secondary Heads Association.

Sheeran, Y. and Barnes, D. (1991) *School Writing*. Milton Keynes. Open University Press.

Shipman, M. (1983) *Assessment in Primary and Middle Schools*. Kent. Croom Helm.

Shulman, L. (1986) Those who understand: knowledge growth in teaching. *Educational Researcher*, 15(2): 4-14.

Siedentrop, D. and Tannehill, D. (2000) (4th ed.) *Developing Teaching Skills in Physical Education*. Mountain View, CA. Mayfield.

Skinner, B.F. (1968) *The Technology of Teaching*. New York. Appleton-Century Crofts.

Smith, J. (2002) *The Learning Game: A Teacher's Inspirational Story*. London. Abacus.

Stakes, R. and Hornby, G. (2000) (2nd ed.) *Meeting Special Needs in Mainstream Schools: A Practical Guide for Teachers*. London. David Fulton.

Stenhouse, L. (1975) *An Introduction to Curriculum Research and Development*. Oxford. Heinemann.

Sternberg, R. J. (1997) *Thinking Styles*. Cambridge. Cambridge University Press.

Stevenson, R. J. and Palmer, J. A. (1994). *Learning Principles, Processes, and Practices*. London. Cassell.

Taber, K. (2001) The mismatch between assumed prior knowledge and the learners' conceptions: a typology of learning impediments. *Educational Studies*, 27(2): 159-171.

Task Group on Assessment and Testing (TGAT) (1988) *National Curriculum, Report*. London. DES.

Terwel, J. (1999) Constructivism and its implications for curriculum theory and practice. *Journal of Curriculum Studies*, 31(2), 195-199.

Tooley, J. and Darby, D. (1998) *Educational Research - A Critique*. London. Ofsted.

Tuckey, C. (1992) Who is a scientist?: children's drawings reveal all. *Education 3-13*, 20, 2, 30-32.

Tyler, R. (1949) *Basic Principles of Curriculum and Instruction*. Chicago. University of Chicago Press.

Van Zwanenberg, N., Wilkinson, L. J. and Anderson, A. (2000) Felder and Silverman's index of learning and Mumford's learning styles questionnaire: how do they compare and do they predict academic performance? *Educational Psychologist*, 20(3), 365-380.

Verkasalo, M., Toumivaara, P. and Lindeman, M. (1996) 15-year-old pupils' and their teachers' values, and their beliefs about the values of an ideal pupil. *Educational Psychology*, 16, 1, 35-47.

Vygotsky, L. S. (1962) *Thought and Language*. Cambridge, MA. MIT Press.

Walker, C. and Newman, I. (1995) What teachers believe. *Educational Research*, 37, 2, 191-202.

Weber, S. and Mitchell, C. (1996) Drawing ourselves into teaching: studying the images that shape and distort teacher education. *Teaching and Teacher Education*, 12, 3, 303-313.

Wetton, N. and McWhirter, J. (1988) Images and curriculum development in health education, in J. Prosser (ed.) *Image-Based Research: A Source Book for Qualitative Researchers*. Brighton: Falmer Press.

Wiliam, D., Askew, M., Rhodes, V., Brown, M. and Johnson, D. (1998) Discover, transmit or connect? Approaches to teaching numeracy in primary schools, *Equals*, Summer 1998.

Wood, D. (1998) *How Children Think and Learn* (2nd ed.). Oxford. Blackwell.

Wray, D. (1999) Teaching literacy: the foundation of good practice. *Education 3-13*, March 1999.

Wray. D. (2001) Literacy in the Secondary School, in *Reading*.

Wray, D. and Lewis, M. (1997) *Extending Literacy: Children Reading and Writing Non-Fiction*. London. Routledge.

Young, M. and Lucas, N. (1999) Pedagogy in further education: new contexts, new theories and new possibilities in P. Mortimore (ed.) *Understanding Pedagogy and its Impact on Learning*. London. Paul Chapman.

ACHIEVING QTS

The Achieving QTS series now includes over 20 titles, encompassing *Audit and Test*, *Knowledge and Understanding*, *Teaching Theory and Practice* and *Skills Tests* titles. The series also has two sub-series — the *Reflective Readers* and the *Practical Handbooks*. As well as covering the core primary subject areas, the series addresses issues of teaching and learning, and of theory and practice, across both primary curriculum and secondary phases. You can find more information on each of these titles on our website: www.learningmatters.co.uk

Assessment for Learning and Teaching in Primary Schools
Mary Briggs, Peter Swatton, Cynthia Martin and Angela Woodfield
176pp ISBN-13: 978 1 903300 74 9 ISBN-10: 1 903300 74 6

Primary English
Audit and Test (second edition)
Doreen Challen
64pp ISBN-13: 978 1 903300 86 2 ISBN-10: 1 903300 86 X

Primary Mathematics
Audit and Test (second edition)
Claire Mooney and Mike Fletcher
52pp ISBN-13: 978 1 903300 87 9 ISBN-10: 1 903300 87 8

Primary Science
Audit and Test (second edition)
John Sharp and Jenny Byrne
80pp ISBN-13: 978 1 903300 88 6 ISBN-10: 1 903300 88 6

Learning and Teaching in Secondary Schools (second edition)
Edited by Viv Ellis
176pp ISBN-13: 978 1 84445 004 6 ISBN-10: 1 84445 004 X

Passing the ICT Skills Test (second edition)
Clive Ferrigan
80pp ISBN-13: 978 1 84445 028 2 ISBN-10: 1 84445 028 7

Passing the Literacy Skills Test
Jim Johnson
80pp ISBN-13: 978 1 903300 12 1 ISBN-10: 1 903300 12 6

Passing the Numeracy Skills Test (third edition)
Mark Patmore
64pp ISBN-13: 978 1 903300 94 7 ISBN-10: 1 903300 94 0

Primary English: Knowledge and Understanding (second edition)
David Wray, Jane Medwell, George Moore and Vivienne Griffiths
224pp ISBN-13: 978 1 903300 53 4 ISBN-10: 1 903300 53 3

Primary English: Teaching Theory and Practice (second edition)
David Wray, Jane Medwell, Hilary Minns, Elizabeth Coates and Vivienne Griffiths
192pp ISBN-13: 978 1 903300 54 1 ISBN-10: 1 903300 54 1

Primary ICT: Knowledge, Understanding and Practice (second edition)
Jane Sharp, Avril Loveless, John Potter and Jonathan Allen
256pp ISBN-13: 978 1 903300 59 6 ISBN-10: 1 903300 59 2

Primary Mathematics: Knowledge and Understanding (second edition)
Claire Mooney, Lindsey Ferrie, Sue Fox, Alice Hansen and Reg Wrathmell
176pp ISBN-13: 978 1 903300 55 8 ISBN-10: 1 903300 55 X

Primary Mathematics: Teaching Theory and Practice (second edition)
Claire Mooney, Mike Fletcher, Mary Briggs and Judith McCullouch
192pp ISBN-13: 978 1 903300 56 5 ISBN-10: 1 903300 56 8

Primary Science: Knowledge and Understanding (second edition)
Rob Johnsey, John Sharp, Graham Peacock and Debbie Wright
232pp   ISBN-13: 978 1 903300 57 2   ISBN-10: 1 903300 57 6

Primary Science: Teaching Theory and Practice (second edition)
John Sharp, Graham Peacock, Rob Johnsey, Shirley Simon and Robin Smith
140pp   ISBN-13: 978 1 903300 58 9   ISBN-10: 1 903300 58 4

Professional Studies: Primary Phase (second edition)
Kate Jacques and Rob Hyland
224pp   ISBN-13: 978 1 903300 60 2   ISBN-10: 1 903300 60 6

Teaching Arts in Primary Schools
Stephanie Penny, Susan Young, Raywen Ford and Lawry Price
192pp   ISBN-13: 978 1 903300 35 0   ISBN-10: 1 903300 35 5

Teaching Citizenship in Primary Schools
Hilary Claire
160pp   ISBN-13: 978 1 84445 010 7   ISBN-10: 1 84445 010 4

Teaching Foundation Stage
Edited by Iris Keating
200pp   ISBN-13: 978 1 903300 33 6   ISBN-10: 1 903300 33 9

Teaching Humanities in Primary Schools
Pat Hoodless, Sue Bermingham, Elaine McCreery and Paul Bowen
192pp   ISBN-13: 978 1 903300 36 7   ISBN-10: 1 903300 36 3

ACHIEVING QTS: REFLECTIVE READERS

Reflective Reader: Primary Professional Studies
Sue Kendall-Seatter
160pp   ISBN-13: 978 1 84445 033 6 ISBN-10: 1 84445 033 3

Reflective Reader: Secondary Professional Studies
Simon Hoult
160pp   ISBN-13: 978 1 84445 034 3 ISBN-10: 1 84445 034 1

Reflective Reader: Primary English
Andrew Lambirth
128pp   ISBN-13: 978 1 84445 035 0   ISBN-10: 1 84445 035 X

Reflective Reader: Primary Mathematics
Louise O'Sullivan, Andrew Harris, Margaret Sangster, Jon Wild, Gina Donaldson and Gill Bottle
128pp   ISBN-13: 978 1 84445 036 7   ISBN-10: 1 84445 036 8

Reflective Reader: Primary Science
Judith Roden
128pp   ISBN-13: 978 1 84445 037 4   ISBN-10: 1 84445 037 6

Reflective Reader: Primary Special Educational Needs
Sue Soan
128pp   ISBN-13: 978 1 84445 038 1   ISBN-10: 1 84445 038 4

ACHIEVING QTS: PRACTICAL HANDBOOKS

Successful Teaching Placement: Primary and Early Years
Jane Medwell
128pp   ISBN-13: 978 1 903300 92 3   ISBN-10: 1 903300 92 4

To order please phone our order line 0845 230 9000 or send an official order or cheque to
BEBC, Albion Close, Parkstone, Poole, BH12 3LL
Order online at www.learningmatters.co.uk